Dedicated to the intrepid devotees of theatre who have gathered under the open sky for story, dance and song since the dawn of history.

Authors:

Dr. Michael Hardy, Director, Institute of Outdoor Theatre
Dr. David Weiss, Professor Emeritus, University of Virginia-Charlottesville
Robert Long, ASTC, Principal, Theatre Consultants Collaborative
Barry Moore, FAIA, Architect and Senior Associate, Gensler, Houston
Christopher Hardy, RLA, CA, Landscape Architect, SWA Group, San Francisco
Scott Parker, Director Emeritus, Institute of Outdoor Theatre

Book Design: Christopher Hardy
Copy Editing & Index: Hilary Weiss Swinson
Front Cover, Regent's Park Open Air Theatre (see Fig. 53)

Third Printing, 2018
ISBN 978-0-692-17850-8

(Previous Editions 978-0-9758874-4-8 and 978-1-4951-1178-5)
Copyright © 2018 by the Southeastern Theatre Conference, Inc.
Greensboro, North Carolina

Acknowledgments

The writing and research team assembled for this project combined many years of experience in theatre, architecture, design, and construction. Several of us had worked together previously, and each brought a unique perspective to the various issues of planning and creating great outdoor theatre spaces. With no shortage of strong opinions, our meetings were lively and the red ink flowed liberally after each successive draft arrived. In the process, we all discovered something new about our subject, and we hope that this end product is richer as a result.

I want to personally thank David, Barry, Robert, Chris and Scott for their time, talent and tenacity in pulling together the information, recommendations and examples used in the book. Our Institute's Business Manager, Susan Phillips, and graduate assistant Adam Parison also helped immensely in the editing. Finally we wish to express our gratitude to the foundation that funded our project. It wishes to remain anonymous but awarded the research grant in honor of two of our team members: David Weiss and Scott Parker.

~Michael Hardy

Foreword

In 2017 the Institute of Outdoor Theatre moved from East Carolina University to become part of the Southeastern Theatre Conference (SETC). Our organizations had worked closely together over the years, and SETC was delighted to welcome the Institute into our organization where its programs would continue to support the field of outdoor theatre. We consider this book a particularly important accomplishment of the Institute, and we are pleased to publish this third edition of it.

Since the book first came out, it has been purchased by theatre planners and architects from all over the world; and it remains, so far as we know, the only work on its subject. Community groups in particular have contacted our office for copies in connection with our consulting program that conducts feasibility studies and theatre planning projects.

We hope you will enjoy the rich pictorial examples of theatres from around the world and benefit from the collective knowledge and experience of its authors.

~Betsey Horth
Executive Director, SETC

Third Edition Note

As our book illustrates, there are many different sizes and styles of outdoor theatre facilities. From the business point of view, there are also several different models of theatre organizations and combinations of those models. When we study a new or existing outdoor venue, it is important for us to figure out exactly what kind of theatre the client really has in mind. An "amphitheatre" can mean anything from 20,000 seats to a few hundred, and business plans range from highly profitable ventures to others that require subsidy. Our projects often involve developing a management plan as well as considering the site, scale, and design of the facility itself.

To do this we begin by learning about the organization's expectations and ascertaining which business model is most likely to fulfill them. Although each result is in some ways unique, we begin by looking at the kinds of existing models that most closely resemble the organization's interests. We generally find that there four types of outdoor theatre businesses:

1. Commercial Venues, Sheds, or Pavilions
2. Passive Park Facilities
3. Mission-Driven Theatres
4. Complementary Attractions

Commercial Venues, Sheds or Pavilions

The primary purpose of these theatres is to make a significant profit by entertaining thousands of visitors who will park, buy tickets and consume concessions. They can range in size from a few thousand seats to over 20,000. They are usually managed by companies like Live Nation, SMG, or AEG, booking their product through promoters and agencies. The attractions that perform in these venues are strong draws: stars or bands who can command high ticket prices for large audiences. Examples of such venues include the Red Rocks Amphitheatre in Denver, River Bend in Cincinnati, and Hollywood Bowl in Los Angeles. This is the only model specifically intended to be profitable. It may be structured as a non-profit organization, but it generates sizeable surpluses. The remaining three types are either non-profit or government-sponsored ventures that usually require different degrees of subsidy.

Passive Park Facility

These theatres are often the simplest types of facilities and may have no equipment other than a few electrical outlets. Groups can perform by signing up with the park on which they are sited or just spontaneously showing up. Park policy may prohibit selling tickets or allow passing the hat for contributions. The main purpose is to add to the quality of life in a community by providing another type of recreation, along with ball fields and playground equipment. The cost of constructing, maintaining and cleaning these facilities is carried in the parks and recreation budget of the local government, and that department also handles scheduling. Any park with a band shell or a concrete slab or raised platform for performances is an example of this type of outdoor theatre. In a common hybrid of this model, the park invites a local theatre company to produce its work on the grounds for some financial consideration or out of tradition or both. The park is still a relatively passive partner except for grounds keeping support, and the theatre assumes the risk of producing the work. Examples are the Public Theatre's Delacorte Theater in New York's Central Park, Delaware Shakespeare in Buffalo's Rockwood Park, and Commonwealth Shakespeare on the Boston Common. The site is a park, but the theatre companies are in the next category: Mission-Driven.

Mission-Driven Theatre

This type of theatre is organized around a mission: artistic, historical, community service, educational, religious, social or some combination of these. It is usually incorporated as a 501(c)(3) non-profit organization. It may also have secondary purposes such as being a tourist attraction or bringing visitors to the downtown, but its programmatic profile is informed by the primary mission. These theatres can produce their own work, or present traveling attractions, or both. Where profit is the purpose of the Commercial Venue and community service the rationale for the Park Facility, the performance itself is central to the Mission-Driven Theatre. These theatres may earn a significant portion of their expenses (up to 50-80%) from ticket sales, concessions and parking. The remainder of their revenue is obtained through fundraising, sponsorships, or in-kind contributions from partners or hosts. This type of theatre usually has a well-developed facility for producing or presenting a variety of types of events and a full-time staff plus additional extra-help brought in during the summer. They frequently also have an indoor winter home. Shakespeare festivals, opera and musical comedies, historical dramas, religious pageants and the full range of music, dance and drama touring events can all be found in Mission-Driven Theatres.

Complementary Attractions

Facilities created for this type of performance are designed to add appeal and marketability to a larger business such as a mall, downtown area, or resort. The primary purpose of the theatre is not to make money, but to attract customers or buyers and entertain visitors, residents and shoppers for the benefit of the host business. These events may be ticketed or free to the public. Theatre facilities in this category can be simple or quite complex, presenting local talent or first-class artists. Their facilities also have a wide range of production capabilities. Food and beverages are usually available as much to enhance the audience experience as to generate revenue. The host business or developer subsidizes the costs of these facilities and performances as part of its cost of doing business. An amphitheatre or stage by a fountain in a shopping mall, a food court with a stage, or a high-end residential development or resort with an amphitheatre are examples of this model. While the scale of operations varies considerably, the business purpose is consistent. There are many variations and hybrids between and within these models, but a successful theatre will tend to be primarily one type with some characteristics of the others. For the architect, planner, or community group wishing to plan a new theatre, it helps to begin with a consideration not only of the facility, but also its purpose.

Michael Hardy
SETC Theatre Consulting Network

1 Introduction 7
Outdoor Theatre Typologies 10
Performance Planning 12

2 Site 15
Site Design Principles 17
An Owner's Guide to Site Selection 18
Potentially Serious Problems 19
Variables to Consider 20
Potential Assets 22
Cost-Effective Landscape Design 24
Stewardship 25

3 Facility 27
Front-of-House Requirements 28
Stage and Backstage Requirements 38

4 Performance Equipment 47
Lighting 48
Sound and Communication 49
Rigging 50
Stage Draperies 51
Design and Procurement 52
Off-Season Storage 52

5 Types of Outdoor Theatres   55

Five Models 56
Types of Outdoor Theatres 57
Model #1: Open Stage with Open Amphitheatre 58
Model #2: Roofed Stage with Open Amphitheatre 74
Model #3: Roofed Stage and Amphitheatre 82
Model #4: Temporary Theatres 98
Model #5: Hybrid Theatres 104
Site-Specific Productions 114

6 Designing and Building a New Theatre   119

The Client and Design Team 120
Phases of Design and Construction 122
Opening the Facility 127

7 Conclusions   129

8 Appendices & Index   133

Appendix A: Further Notes on Design and Construction Process 134
Appendix B: Schedule for a Typical 1,000 - Seat Outdoor Theatre 135
Appendix C: Image Sources and Attributions 138
Index 140

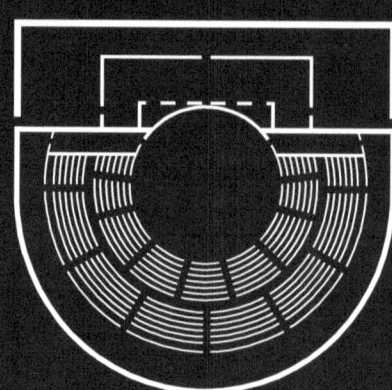

Chapter 1

Introduction

Introduction

Theatre has been performed outdoors for thousands of years. Indeed, the entire field of the performing arts originated in ceremonies, rituals and re-enactments conducted under an open sky. Over time, the performances became more specialized and complex with playwrights, trained performers and designers. Outdoor theatre facilities have also existed for thousands of years, with the most familiar types being Greek and Roman amphitheatres, the Spanish corrales and the Elizabethan public theatres such as the Globe and the Rose. The classic open stage and amphitheatre design, in particular, has continued to exert a dominant influence on the architecture of many contemporary outdoor performance spaces around the world.

Outdoor performances of all kinds continue to be produced today. These include religious and historical plays, Shakespeare festivals, musical and dramatic plays, dance and musical concerts of all kinds. In fact, the number of all outdoor performances taken together has never been greater. Over the past 50 years, the Institute of Outdoor Theatre (IOT) has conducted over 60 feasibility studies for new theatre facilities and organizations. We have advised numerous communities and organizations on artistic, technical, architectural and management best practices. The IOT's mission is to support outdoor theatre organizations, and to this end we study market trends and demographic shifts and solicit field reports on the status and health of outdoor theatres in the United States and abroad.

Fig 1 / The Theatre of Dionysus Eleuthereus in Athens is one of the earliest of the Greek theatres preserved, the current configuration dating to the third century BCE. The original purpose was for religious drama, being used for festivals in honor of the god Dionysus. Many properties of the layout, including riser seating, thrust stage and acoustics, are still evident in many contemporary outdoor amphitheatre designs.

We have noticed a trend over the past ten years that many theatres are experiencing a serious decline in their audiences. The Institute has been studying this through consulting actively with our member theatres and conducting annual attendance and audience opinion surveys. In the process we have identified a number of contributing factors such as changing audience expectations, programming challenges, increased competition from other live attractions, the rise of digital content and, of course, the weather. But there is one area where we find that some theatres have been more successful than others in structuring a programming and attendance experience that keeps their organizations competitive: the theatre facility itself.

Based on this observation, the IOT assembled a team of experienced architects, theatre consultants, designers and managers who have worked in the field for many years. We have surveyed and analyzed the different types of outdoor theatre facilities in operation today, and we publish this guide to share that information with current and future theatre planners and builders. Our findings have led us to change some of the basic recommendations for outdoor theatre design that we have made for the past 50 years. These new best practices and recommendations are explained in this report, serving as a guide for theatre companies, community organizations, non-profits or city planners interested in building new outdoor theatre facilities or refurbishing existing facilities.

Fig 2 / The Roman Theatre at Bosra in Syria was built in the second century CE. It is the largest and best preserved of all the Roman theatres in the Middle East. The dramatic evolution of the backdrop, set and wings during the 500 years since the original Greek theatres reflects a growing complexity of production and spectacle.

Our guide does not replace the necessary skills and talents of a complete theatre design team collaborating to create a successful space for its unique vision. That team should include building and landscape architects, theatre consultants, and engineers working with civic organizations, theatre production groups and boards of directors. Our text is, rather, a starting point: a critical survey of the different possibilities and a reminder of the essential elements that are needed to create a successful theatre facility today and for the future.

Outdoor Theatre Typologies

In this guide we will review the basic characteristics and requirements of a theatre's facility, equipment, and site followed by a specific description of five different models of outdoor theatres.

The types are:

1. Open Stage with Open Amphitheatre
2. Roofed Stage with Open Amphitheatre
3. Roofed Stage and Amphitheatre
4. Temporary Theatres
5. Hybrid Theatres

Each type has specific advantages and disadvantages and some, such as temporary theatres and hybrids, are defined by specific examples rather than a firm set of rules. Where historic precedents occur for these types of theatres, we point that out and show examples. We have included photographs of actual contemporary theatres for each type as well as illustrated schematic designs where appropriate. Issues related to the landscaping and site plans are also discussed.

We have somewhat arbitrarily selected a theatre size of 1,000 audience seats for our illustrations. Conceptually, the types are certainly scalable for anything from a few hundred seats up to 2,000 or more. The quantity and space needed for audience amenities (restrooms, parking spaces, concessions, pavilion capacity, etc.) will vary according to how many people must be accommodated. The key element to consider in determining the capacity for a specific theatre is the balance between the ability to generate revenue from ticket sales and the cost of construction. A theatre that routinely fails to sell 50% of its seats is too large, while one that always sells out will wish it were larger. There is no scientific method for determining the perfect count, and the best approach may be to plan somewhat conservatively, leaving room for future expansion. Outdoor facilities have an advantage for planning for expansion in contrast to indoor facilities. If expansion is planned for in the initial facility design, informal space, such as a picnic meadow uphill of the structured seating, can double as spill-over space while the company cultivates its attendance. We have noticed a trend for smaller, more intimate spaces for dramas and historical plays, and larger civic-scaled spaces for mixed-venue theatres supporting a range of theatre and musical programs. Right-sizing is one of the services an IOT feasibility study can provide.

This guide is intended to assist organizations and their design teams when they are at the very beginning of the process to plan, design and build their own new theatres or renovate existing ones. We hope that these examples will help bring new ideas into those early discussions and decisions, and that the planners will be encouraged to design practical, functional and exciting theatres that will enrich their communities and arts organizations for years to come.

Open Stage with Open Amphitheatre

Roofed Stage with Open Amphitheatre

Roofed Stage and Amphitheatre

Temporary Theatres

Hybrid Theatres

Performance Planning

Before discussing the specific issues of theatre design a theatre organization needs to begin by determining what is going to be performed on the stage and a realistic expectation of how many people will come to see what is being offered. While this sounds obvious, many of the more serious problems in outdoor theatre stem from the failure to adequately consider these two factors. Older theatre establishments may have originally had valid plans, but changing times and presentations may have left their facilities or programs obsolete or in need of renovation.

Outdoor theatres present special challenges for both performers and audiences, including the fact that the seasons and weather dictate when a facility can be used. For an outdoor theatre to utilize its seasonal window of opportunity most effectively, it needs to have strong enough performances to compete with other available attractions. A varied selection of performances can help appeal to the widest possible audience and encourage repeat attendance. Theatres scheduling a variety of events require more adaptable stage and backstage facilities than those presenting only a few productions each season.

Some outdoor theatre companies may offer only one signature production, having produced that show for decades. When these facilities opened, they were often one of the few entertainment options in that area and enjoyed little competition. Today these theatres tend to suffer more than others from declining audiences. Their original production may have become stale and may need to be reinvented in a way that reflects modern tastes and interests. In addition, even in rural places digital entertainment is readily accessible and cheap. To counter this competition, shows must adapt, providing an authentic compelling experience. In some cases, the original play might be simply supplemented with additional productions and performances. This strategy is being employed by several single-show organizations, but their single-purpose theatre structures can frustrate that diversification.

The different types of outdoor productions generally fall into the four categories of Shakespeare Festivals, Religious Plays, History Plays and Variety Theatre (producing musicals and plays). The religious and history plays typically have the 'one production' dilemma referred to above, while the Shakespeare and variety theatres produce several different shows by definition. All of them, however, share the issues of how to protect their performers and audiences from the weather and how to achieve a high quality of physical production (scenery, costumes, lighting and sound) outdoors. The majority of this study will deal with these common challenges and the pros and cons of different types of outdoor theatre facilities for addressing them.

Before leaving the subject of programming, however, a distinction should be made between producing and presenting. When a show is produced, the producing organization casts, rehearses and builds the production from the ground up. The typical outdoor production requires at least two or three weeks of preparation (even more for a new production) to accomplish this before performing for audiences. There are two methods used for producing more than one show in a season. The most efficient (and exhausting) model is *summer stock* in which a show performs for one week, during which the next show is rehearsed, and so on through the summer. Summer stock theatres producing as many as five to ten plays over as many weeks in this manner are less common than in the past, but they are still viable organizations. The second multiple-production model is *repertory* in which several shows run throughout a season, alternating on different nights. Repertory generally involves a single company of performers playing different roles in the different shows. Repertory rehearsals can happen before any of the shows open or be staggered like stock, with the productions added into the rotation when they are ready. However producing is done, it is a time-consuming effort both artistically and technically.

Presenting is a different process in which a theatre pays a fee for a performance that has been created somewhere else and is on tour. A show or performance can be presented anytime a theatre is empty and the show is available in the area. The types of performances that tour are primarily musical events, comedy shows, dance concerts and children's shows. Theatre companies also tour, but much less frequently than the other types. The advantage of presenting is that the theatre doesn't have to do anything on the artistic side except make a sound judgment on what will appeal to its audience. Most of the other functions of running a theatre are exactly the same as they are in producing. The 'art of presenting' is the art of selecting good shows, negotiating appropriate contracts, selling tickets and building a strong reputation.

Theatre facilities tend to be designed for organizations that plan either to produce or to present. Outdoor theatres often successfully combine both types of programming. The typical outdoor theatre has three potential seasons:

- The main summer season when weather is best for tourism and outdoor activities throughout the week
- The late spring 'shoulder season' when audiences tend to be more regional and weekend events conflict less with their school and work schedules
- The post-summer shoulder season, which is also more weekend oriented

During the summer season, the producing model can take advantage of the week-long schedule and the tourism potential that may exist in some areas, with occasional presentations filling in any dark days. In the shoulder seasons, the presenting model with only one or two performances will be best for the weekend schedules and needs of a local audience for variety. If an organization wishes to utilize this type of business model, it will need a different kind of theatre than the one that only produces one or two shows during the summer season.

The important link between programming and theatre design is discussed more specifically as we review the different types of outdoor theatres operating today.

Chapter 2

Site

The Site

In the late 1800's landscape architects Jens Jensen, Frank A. Waugh and John Howard began designing and promoting public outdoor theatre facilities. As outdoor theatre performance evolved in the early 20th century, the design and context of the site remained an integral part of the productions. Prior to the current era of public outdoor theatres, outdoor theatre facilities were largely either informal (placed for convenience for their productions) or formal private theatres (usually on set-aside portions of estates). For many years amphitheatre designers looked to classical inspiration for the facility and the grounds. The difference for the early performance company–operated theatres, like Oberammergau, Germany, was that the landscape became an integral part of the scenery. This site-specific character was embraced by the outdoor historical theatre movement, with stories relying on features in the landscape and the history of the place to immerse patrons in the experience. The historical plays enabled outdoor theatre and landscape design to break from classicism, to express the periods of the plays' subjects.

Today's outdoor theatre facilities, whether historical plays, rotating shows, public amphitheatres, or grounds for temporary theatres, inherit this unique relationship to their sites that is rich and contrasts to indoor theatres that shut out the world. The site for an outdoor theatre helps tell the story, grounding the tragedy and comedy to place, enriching community and local cultural identity.

The site and grounds of an outdoor theatre facility are a major influence on the quality of the experience of a show. Because of being outdoors, the facility will have many uncontrolled variables that can either be a detriment or boon to the experience. Weather, wildlife, insects, wind, noise pollution, undesirable views and other factors can all break the attention of the audience and distract from the story. Alternatively, directed views, real trees, larger bodies of water, fire and stars can all create an experience impossible in a theatre hall. Careful site design and proper maintenance can make the theatre experience comfortable, cultural and unique.

The site can also have major implications to the costs of building and maintaining a facility. This chapter provides an overview of site-related issues for the owners and operators of outdoor theatres. These concepts are presented in a manner to aid the owner in asking the right questions and securing the right consultants to successfully implement and maintain the site for a new outdoor theatre.

Fig 3 / The longest running outdoor drama is a passion play, first performed in 1634 in Oberammergau, Bavaria. The play came about from a vow to produce a play of the life and death of Jesus, forever after, if the village was spared the devastation of the plague. When the death rate dropped in 1633, the community pulled the production together and started the tradition. Now the village produces the play for one season every ten years.

Site Design Principles

When considering the design and building of a new outdoor theatre facility, incorporating the site characteristics into the design process can help take advantage of the natural assets and liabilities of the site. Perhaps there is a key boulder that the stage could be built around, or a low area that could be made into a pond. A few specific ideas are useful for having preliminary discussions with design professionals regarding the site of an outdoor theatre:

- *Genius loci*: Literally the spirit of a place. What is it about this site that is special and unique?
- Place-making: The craft of creating a distinctive, recognizable and memorable social space. How will this place be memorable, and how will people inhabit the space?
- Character: The character of the landscape is often a sum of its components and context. The character can also be guided by the design. Is this site to complement the surrounding mountains with an 'alpine meadow feel'? Is this site to be a green oasis in an urban jungle?
- Topography and aspect: The shape of terrain and direction of the slopes. Is there a hill with a broad northern exposure? Is this a flat site that will require major grading or structure to make a riser? Where is the sun in relation to the stage and audience viewpoint?
- Circulation: The movement of people and vehicles to and through the site. What is the experience along this journey; how do people move from their car or bus to their seats?
- Experiential design: Designing to anticipate the full experience of the visitor. When do we want the visitors to leave the world behind for this theatre experience? Is it after the ticket booth? In the lobby? The parking lot? At the gate? How do we choreograph their experience?

Fig 4 / The Scott Outdoor Amphitheater is the heart of Swarthmore College, where students begin and end their college experience. The amphitheater was designed by Thomas W. Sears. In addition to freshman orientation and commencement, concerts, dance and theatre productions are held under the canopy of tulip poplars and white oaks.

Fig 5/ Sigmund Stern Recreation Grove in San Francisco, California, hosts a variety of events, including the annual Stern Grove Festival. Landscape architect Lawrence Halprin sought 'To create a mystical place where one would be inspired to reach into oneself.'

Fig 6/ Cemil Topuzlu Open-Air Theatre in Istanbul, Turkey. The amphitheatre, designed by architects Nihad Yücel and Nahid Uysal, takes advantage of pre-existing topography and embraces the city beyond as a backdrop.

An Owner's Guide to Site Selection

In the design and development of a new outdoor theatre, a skilled owner's representative well-versed in related construction projects and regional construction policies is an invaluable asset to a development team. There are times, however, when a full-time owner's representative is not available. Sometimes it is necessary to keep the management team lean, and have the owner directly manage the project. In these situations part-time contracts with construction management or architecture firms may be preferred.

In all cases, an informed owner can vastly improve the quality, mitigate the risks and reduce the costs of a project. It is important for this individual to understand the chain of responsibility of the design and construction process, and how he/she can best direct the process. The owner must always remember all the consultants and contractors are ultimately accountable to them. The following description of site selection includes notes for opportunities for the owner and development team to achieve cost savings and quality control. For the purposes of this description, the owner, owner's representative, developer, or project manager will be referred to collectively as the 'client'.

Choosing a Site

Temporary and portable theatres can adapt to a range of sites. For more permanent outdoor theatres, the right site can be as important to the cost of construction and success of the show as the facility program. Marketing and feasibility studies can evaluate proposed sites as one of many factors for determining the viability of a show—these studies are best conducted prior to purchasing or leasing a site for a show. Probable visitor counts may vary based on a site's relationship to regional transportation, tourism, vacation homes, or population density.

The characteristics of the site can also have major implications for the costs of construction and maintenance. Ideally, a licensed landscape architect, environmental engineer, or civil engineer will be contracted to assist in determining the right site, in addition to a real estate professional. Regardless of the team evaluating the site, there are key variables to consider.

Fig 7/ Even though some sites may seem like an amazing deal, the characteristics of a site can have major implications to the cost of building an outdoor theatre.

Potentially Serious Problems

Wetlands
Registered wetlands are protected under federal and state laws. Filling wetlands without a permit can trigger massive fines from the state and the Environmental Protection Agency (EPA), and can easily bankrupt a smaller development organization. Wetlands can be a scenic and ecological asset for a site, as long as they are not impacted by the proposed development. When evaluating a site, the owner should already have a concept of the area requirements for the proposed theatre, support facilities, and parking requirements. If there are wetlands on a site, first evaluate if the proposed improvements can be laid out in a manner to maintain an adequate buffer of undisturbed land around the wetlands.

Shallow Bedrock
When grading a site to accommodate the roads and foundations necessary for an outdoor theatre, the presence of bedrock can massively increase construction costs. At the same time, bedrock 3' or more beneath finish grade can be a major structural asset. Building on exposed rock can be very expensive.

Expansive Soil
Swelling clay soils create a variety of challenges for construction, and can often cause the failure of small building foundations, sidewalks and retaining walls. A soil test for a site (best done with multiple samples from across the development zone) will be able to determine if the soils are expansive. Most earthwork contractors and landscape architects should be able to tell simply by the texture of the soil in their palm. Both soil conditions and bedrock can be easily determined or mitigated with the help of a geotechnical report, which will be discussed later.

Overly Steep or Overly Flat Sites
Sites on either extreme of topography, whether steep or flat, will require greater costs in grading and drainage systems. Sites with average slopes steeper than 3:1 may seem appealing for the laying out of an amphitheatre, but are expensive and unsuitable for parking or roadways. Sites that have less than 2% slope may have poor drainage. Both will require significant investment in grading.

A High Water Table
A high water table can weaken foundations and cause drainage problems, especially if any excavation is required for a stage area or pit. A high water table can significantly increase maintenance costs through requiring sump pumps for drainage.

Flood Plains
The Federal Emergency Management Agency (FEMA) periodically issues flood maps. From the perspective of a client, the most important is the 100-year flood plain. If the theatre is located in a 100-year flood plain, flood insurance rates will be much higher, and in some cases, the property may not be insurable. In recent years, flood plains are changing. What FEMA mapped as 200-year flood planes are sometimes shifting into the 100-year or 50-year zones. This can be easily checked on FEMA's public maps online, or with the local planning or public works departments.

Fig 8 / Understanding site conditions, risks, and adjacencies can prevent unexpected surprises.

Liquefaction Zones

In parts of the country susceptible to earthquakes, liquefaction zones are areas where the soil is unstable in an earthquake. When an earthquake occurs, the soil effectively liquefies, and buildings, walls, and foundations can literally sink into the mud. Construction requirements in liquefaction zones vary by locality but substantially increase the costs of foundations and structure. Liquefaction zones can be found on the United States Geological Survey (USGS) website.

Endangered Species Habitat

In some states the construction of a public facility such as an outdoor theatre will trigger an Environmental Impact Review (EIR) prior to entitlement or permitting. One of the quickest ways to complicate an EIR is if there is any endangered species habitat on the site of the proposed improvements. This can be readily determined either through hiring a biologist to review the site or simply checking with the local department of fish and wildlife.

Incompatible Zoning

If a site is zoned for a different land use, such as single family residential, the client must get a variance to be able to permit and build the facility. Acquiring a variance can draw out the schedule, and there is no guarantee that the variance will go through. Zoning is determined by the local municipal government, and usually only applies to land within city limits. One can find the zoning of a parcel with the local planning or building departments. In many locations, the zoning is written on the title, but zoning maps change over time, and the title may be out of date. All of these variables are surmountable, but it is best to be aware of the potential hidden costs, delays, and conditions of a site prior to leasing or purchasing.

Variables to Consider

Adjacent Landowners

When picking a site for an outdoor theatre, the client must consider both the current neighbors and zoning, as well as the potential future neighbors for the anticipated life of the facility. Theatres located in a stable built context, such as an urban setting, public park or national park, will be able to better predict their future neighbors and plan the facility's impact on the community. Community impact issues may include noise abatement, traffic management, security, and provision of public space. Getting a sense of the community and the degree of potential NIMBYism (Not-In-My-Back-Yard) before purchasing a site can sometimes save years of headaches. For sites without a defined context—such as surrounding farmland that could become suburbs, ensuring long-term positive relationships with future neighbors can be built into the site design, with buffer zones around the property, grading for noise abatement, and the aspect of the amphitheatre.

Orientation

What direction will the theatre face? In a hot southern climate with anticipated daytime shows, a northeastern orientation for the audience is the coolest aspect. If sunsets are important for the anticipated program, perhaps a northwestern orientation is better. In cold climates a sheltered southern exposure may be best. In addition to comfort, orientation can make a massive impact on the noise attenuation of the facility and audience. Just as amphitheatres can direct an actor's voices up to the audience, the concave amphitheatre can reflect the sound of the audience's applause two or three times beyond the backstage of the amphitheatre. Strong prevailing winds can also have an impact on the theatre's acoustics.

Existing Structures

Are there existing structures on the site and, if so, can they be refurbished or demolished? Abandoned or dilapidated structures can have major cost and liability implications for a construction project, and the client should determine the state of any existing structures, potential hazardous materials and demolition costs, and build those costs into the offer. Abandoned buildings that remain are difficult to ignore, and for facilities attracting families and small children, even fenced-off abandoned buildings can be a temptation for exploration and potential injury.

Hydrology

Hydrology is the movement of water on and below a site, and the existing hydrology can have major implications for the costs and maintenance of the theatre's drainage systems. Are there creeks on a site? If so, what are they like at peak flood? What is the state of the ground water? Are there vernal pools? What is the general direction of the water on the site, and how will the proposed project change this system? Landscape architects, civil engineers, environmental engineers, and hydrologists can all provide hydrological analysis and strategy.

Brownfields

Brownfields are previously disturbed land, usually associated with industrial land use. Brownfields can be a huge potential liability or an asset for an outdoor facility. Many brownfields have contamination issues, such as leaky underground storage tanks, chemical spills and plumes, or asbestos. The Comprehensive Environmental Response, Compensation, and Liability Act (CERCLA) attaches liability for contamination to all parties associated with a property. Without other legal assurances, if a client buys a property that is contaminated, even if the client does not know of the contamination at the time of the purchase, the client is liable for cleanup along with all the past landowners. This law scares many clients away from brownfield redevelopment. At the same time, many states have local brownfield redevelopment laws with liability waivers. In addition, many brownfield sites cannot be developed as residential property due to requiring capping for contamination or other issues. As a result, these properties can be low cost or even free, especially if the proposed development is a public asset, such as an outdoor theatre. If considering a brownfield site, there can be great perks and hidden costs. Hiring a reputable environmental engineer and working closely with the state brownfield redevelopment agency are important for success. In many states, additional funding can be accessed for public facilities to be built on brownfields.

Comfort

Before purchasing a site, consider how comfortable the site is to occupy, and what measures you would want to take to make it more comfortable for audience members. When you visit a site for evaluation, reflect on your experience. Were there billions of mosquitos? Can you smell a local sewer? Does the wind howl on the hilltop? Can you anticipate regular fog? Most uncomfortable site conditions can be mitigated, but should be considered because every additional modification to a site can require time and money.

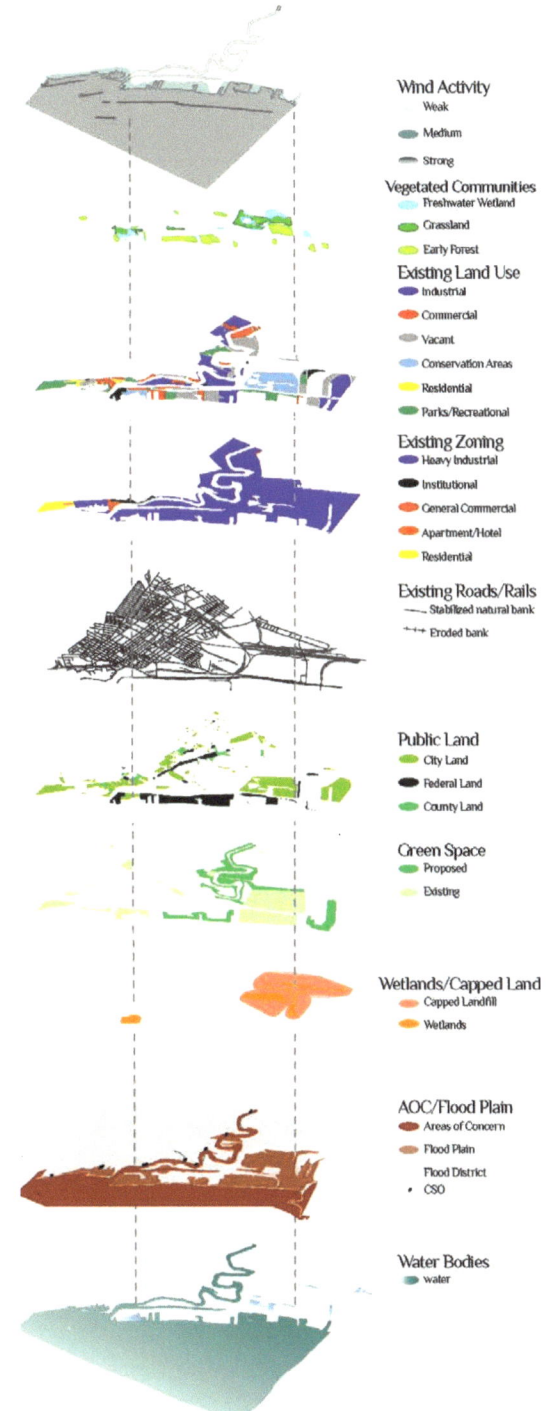

Fig 9 / An exploded axon, showing an example of the many variables to consider when picking a site for a facility.

Potential Assets

Stable Soils
The stability of the soils can halve or double the cos foundations as well as the durability of paved surfaces.

Appropriate Preexisting Grading
If the grading of a site lends itself to the proposed land use, the cost of earthwork can be greatly reduced.

Clear Site
If a site has already been cleared, the cost of tree removals and demolition can be erased. Also, consider the mobilization of construction. Surgical construction around attractive site assets, such as mature trees to remain, does not necessarily mean an increase in cost, as long as the design team develops a realistic mobilization plan.

Stable Surrounding Land Ownership
For facilities that will be occupied for many years, changes to adjacent properties could become a major problem in future years. Sites that are adjacent to or in parklands, protected areas, or stable, established communities are preferable.

Potential Access to Mass Transit
The single biggest carbon cost of outdoor theatres is visitor transportation. Individuals and groups driving private cars to the facility also significantly contribute to the wear and tear of the tarmac, sometimes decreasing resurfacing intervals from 20 years to 10 years or less. In many locations mass transit, other than bus shuttles, is impossible. If mass transportation is a local asset, these costs can be mitigated. If a site is on a transit line from a major urban population, there may also be a strong marketing advantage.

Supportive Community
The local community will change over time, but if the community is supportive at the beginning of a project, all bureaucratic processes around landownership, variances, and permitting will be greatly simplified. A supportive community can assist with grants, volunteer programs, and the general good will that every non-profit ultimately depends upon.

Fig 10 / Especially for public sites, working through a community design process can mitigate NIMBYism and build social capital for the future facility. This perspective shows the results of a public process for Shoelace Park in the Bronx, NY, led by Mathews Nielsen Landscape Architects, P.C. (MNLA) with the Bronx River Alliance. Through community workshops and engaging key stakeholders, MNLA was able to negotiate consensus for the proposed park improvements.

Cost-Effective Landscape Design

Outdoor theatres rarely have generous maintenance budgets, and those budgets are often focused on the structure and health and safety. There are strategies that can be built into the design of the grounds of the facility to ensure a beautiful landscape even with low maintenance budgets.

Low-Impact Design

Low-impact design is the concept of minimizing the disturbance of a site. Many outdoor theatres, such as *Unto These Hills* in Cherokee, NC, or *Texas!* in Canyon, TX, or the Minack Theatre in Cornwall, UK, are sited in beautiful natural environments. *Tecumseh's* theatre includes a pond that is effectively used in the production. Protecting the existing trees and habitat as much as possible during construction reaps rewards when the site is preserved as a healthy dominant forest. To do so, the consultant team can add site protection as a section of the bid documents. Developing a tree preservation plan, phasing mobilizing sites, and sensitive grading can narrow the construction impact to the surgical installation of the intended facility. Depending on how difficult mobilizing becomes, contractors may increase their bids. The cost of site protection is a small upfront cost when compared to trying to plant mature trees. Low-impact design can also have a variety of ancillary benefits such as more wildlife around the facility and reduced flood risks. Low-impact design takes advantage of existing natural resources and systems and is environmentally sensitive.

Low-Maintenance Design

The grounds of the outdoor facility do not have to be a pre-existing forest to be low maintenance. A designed and crafted landscape can also be low-maintenance if it is planned accordingly. If a client values low-maintenance design, they should target landscape architects with pertinent experience during the assembly of the design team. In addition to contract documents and construction administration, most landscape firms also offer an additional service developing operations and maintenance reports. An O&M report is best developed during the design process, as it can anticipate grounds maintenance budgets. The O&M report can include maintenance schedules, anticipated man hours, recommendations for care for different plantings and gardens, a turf management plan, and technical maintenance recommendations for irrigation systems, drainage systems, and lighting. The following is a partial list of low-maintenance design opportunities.

- Native species and adapted species. Planting the site with native species (i.e., species that would naturally live on the site) and adapted species (plants that are adapted to the site conditions) is an important way to save time and money.
- Low water use and xeriscaping. Xeriscaping is designing a landscape that requires no additional water other than what the site naturally receives. Low water use anticipates some irrigation, but either only in unusually dry conditions or during establishment.
- Turf design. Turf is a high-labor and landscape material, but it is also a highly desirable surface for picnicking and play. It is important to have a realistic idea of how the turf will be used. For high-use lawns, intensive maintenance is required for the lawn to continue to perform. For low-use lawns, the turf can be designed for minimal maintenance using low-mow and low-water species. A turf management plan accounts for the anticipated play hours, rest periods, species of grasses, irrigation system, fertilizing plan, and mowing program.
- Resilient materials. Materials that do not or only slowly degrade with time can greatly simplify maintenance. Stone, 316L Stainless Steel, anodized aluminum, black locust timber, and quality concrete are all examples of resilient materials.
- High quality and simple furnishings. When building an outdoor facility to last for generations, the furnishings must take into account the need for replacements. Higher quality furnishings may save long-term budgets through not requiring regular replacement. Simple detailing can make repairs and replacements easier.
- Low energy LED lighting. LED lights have revolutionized the outdoor lighting industry. High-quality LED lights can now provide great color rendering while using a small fraction of the energy of old-fashioned outdoor lamps, such as sodium or halide fixtures. The higher upfront expense is quickly paid for in energy savings and the lifespan of the LEDs.

- Lifetime investments. Quite often it is a far easier task to attract funds for capital investment than for operation costs. As a result, there are many strategies that can be included in the initial design that will have long-term payback. Solar power and water heating, microwind power, microhydro water power, greywater recycling, and geothermal cooling are all strategies that can be costly retrofits, but if built into the initial facility, can greatly reduce a facility's energy and water costs. In 2010, the McGraw-Hill Construction group reported that for the first time, the majority of 'green construction' projects were initiated because of cost savings rather than ethics. Today, most contractors can build LEED Silver facilities with no increase in initial construction cost compared with traditional construction. Building a net-zero facility is possible, and the more energy savings and waste reduction are built into a design, the lower the facility maintenance costs will be in the future.

Stewardship

As Aldo Leopold and Wendell Berry noted, being out in the landscape, being of the landscape, and being a part of a place-based community inspires a land ethic. Outdoor theatres are important cultural landscapes, and as such are great venues to attract and promote stewardship. If an outdoor theatre has a good community relationship and attractive or historic grounds, it is far easier to attract volunteer support than low-quality grounds and poor community relations. Local master gardening groups, Scout troops, schools and churches can all be sources of support. At the same time, a single well-trained maintenance professional assisted by volunteers and seasonal help is well worth the investment – maintenance is cheaper than rebuilding. Dedicated staff are better able to guide volunteers to work productively to maintain the grounds. Creating a culture of stewardship of the place can be recognized by the patrons and become self-perpetuating.

Fig 11 / The Smith-Ritch Point 722-seat outdoor theatre is located along the Guadalupe River in Texas. 'The Point' is the longest-running outdoor theatre in Texas, featuring local volunteers in summer stock. Important to the success of The Point has a been a long-term connection to the local community, with attendance and participation part of local family traditions.

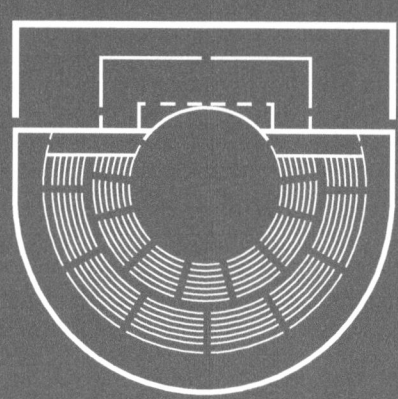

Chapter 3

Facility

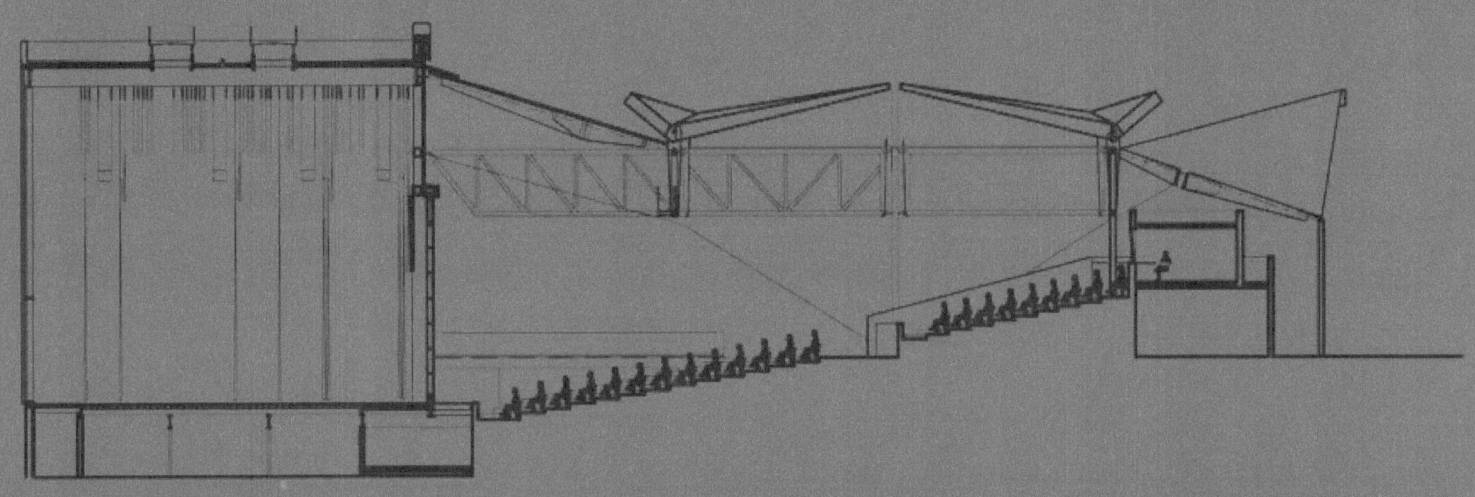

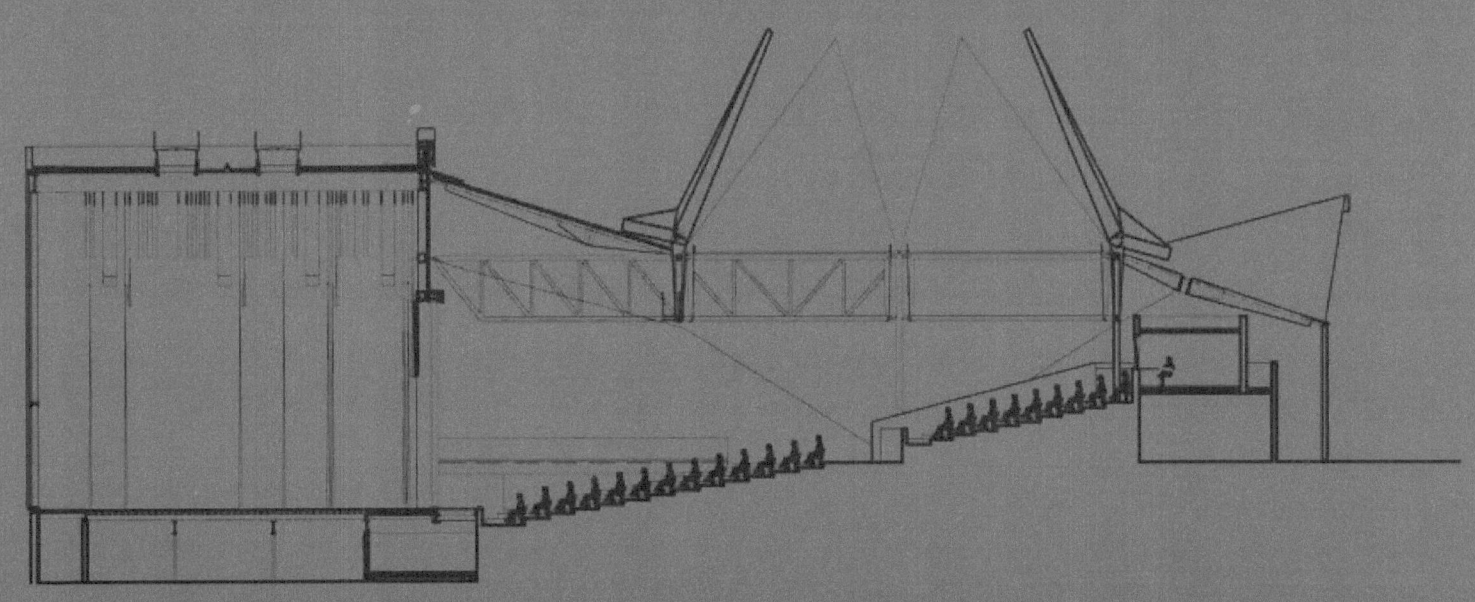

The Facility

As the design process begins on any outdoor theatre facility, the tendency is to focus on the stage and seating areas. There is much beyond these basic elements that must be taken into account, though the needs may vary from one instance to another. This portion of our study will address the most common support rooms and buildings that should be considered in the design process.

Front-of-House Requirements

Arrival

Well-designed directional signage is an important element in the arrival sequence for outdoor theatres and is equally important for all types of facilities, whether in rural areas or in center-city park venues. It is wise to plan the arrival sequence to a theatre with the assumption that everyone coming to the theatre has never been there before. With that as a guiding principle, planners are more likely to ensure that patrons will easily and comfortably find their destination, especially those who have come for the first time.

Once patrons have reached the venue they should see a conspicuous and attractive entrance welcoming them to the evening's event. Just as theatres for many centuries have had marquees and large signs designating the entrance, the facilities should clearly denote, 'This is the Place!' Ideally, the entry should be attractive though it need not be elaborate. Clarity of entry is the key and if the venue has a particular purpose, for instance with a history play, there may be decor in keeping with the nature of the work being presented.

The arrival sequence for outdoor theatres in urban areas may require a different type of directional signage than for rural venues. Outdoor theatre facilities may be located in city parks so large that it will be difficult to locate the facility. In that case signage will be especially important while also requiring careful planning so that the signs are not a nuisance to citizens using the park for other purposes. Whether permanent or not, aids to finding the venue require careful planning from the beginning.

Fig 12 / Historic entrance to *Unto These Hills* at the Mountainside Theatre, Cherokee, NC. The original palisade defined the threshold to the historical drama.

Parking

In almost every case of an outdoor theatre venue, other than in more dense, urban areas with access to public transportation, the patrons will arrive either by car or by bus. These vehicles must be accommodated in an attractive manner with relative convenience to the performance area. A 1,000-seat theatre should provide parking for at least 400 cars, based on the industry standard of 2.5 patrons per car. It can be assumed that approximately an acre will be needed for 100 to 150 cars, depending on the layout. That statistic, however, does not include the devices that will create an attractive parking area, such as tree islands, designated pathways and helpful signage. Additional parking will be needed for performers and staff.

The parking spaces must be located well away from the theatre to avoid distractions during a performance from the sound and light of automobiles, but not so far as to make it difficult for patrons to walk to the theatre itself. Pathways must be comfortable, easily negotiable and well lit. It must be assumed that some patrons may wish to get to the theatre in a wheelchair from the parking lot or they may wish to be dropped off closer to the entry to the theatre. Similarly, buses may wish to drive to the entrance and drop their passengers before heading back to the lot and a parking area well away from the theatre. The design of the site should take into account these variables for circulation, and seek to maximize ease of access while minimizing vehicular queues and idling time.

Once again, however, the urban site may offer different challenges for access. Study of options other than individual automobile parking, such as public transit, bicycles, charter buses, etc., should be taken into account in order to provide the greatest convenience for all members of the audience.

Options for Patrons

In many cases patrons will naturally flow from the parking area to the theatre and settle into their seats. If, however, the venue will regularly attract visitors from beyond the immediate community, various options for giving them some 'extras', so to speak, are worth considering. An 'extra' may consist of a simple park-like area where families or groups might rest for a few moments, with exhibits of one kind or another related to the event they will soon see. This is especially appropriate for Shakespeare festivals and historical plays, but any sort of entertainment can evoke interesting exhibits.

Many of the existing outdoor theatres offer a dining experience, providing dinner before the show at a reasonable cost. This is especially attractive to patrons from another community who don't want to spend time searching for a place to dine before the show. Whether food is offered for purchase at the theatre or not, a few picnic tables may be in order for those who wish to bring their own food.

Yet another option is a small performance area for pre-show entertainment. This need not be elaborate, just a simple platform or open area where a small group of performers can help to get the audience in the mood for the performance they are about to enjoy.

Fig 13 / *The Lost Colony*, Roanoke Island, NC. Beyond facility design, the programming of the entrance enhances the patron's experience. When considering the design of the facility, it is important to plan flexible space for these activities.

These and other possibilities are options that might be selected depending on the intention of the performance venue. They are all worth considering in the process of creating an event. Going to these theatres should be different than walking into a movie house, picking up some popcorn and settling in for a couple of hours of entertainment. Patrons should expect and receive much more. Planning the theatre experience from the time they cross the threshold into the theatre – whether that threshold is in the lobby or at the entrance gate – is important for developing the 'complete experience' that patrons seek from live performance.

Entry Pavilion
Every theatre has a lobby. In the case of outdoor venues the lobby, or pavilion, should also be a place to seek shelter if it rains (for unsheltered outdoor theatres). The pavilion should be large enough to accommodate most of the audience standing up, and should provide adequate space for circulation. The space need not be elaborate, but since it is the point of arrival it should be reasonably attractive as well as readily accessible for people with disabilities. This area may also house several additional spaces and facilities as described below. Depending on the physical and environmental circumstances some of these facilities may be separate structures. The pavilion may also offer a useful location for hanging lighting instruments as described in the text on lighting positions below.

Box Office
The ticket office should be immediately apparent and easily accessible as the patron arrives at the theatre. In some cases tickets are sold near the parking lot, and this is reasonable if the path to the theatre itself is the only way to get to the production. Usually, however, the box office is close to the entry but planned to assure that patrons waiting in line do not obstruct traffic into the theatre. Placing the ticket windows under a roof in case there is a shower is also a good practice.

The size of the box office will be determined by the seating capacity of the amphitheatre but it is always useful to have more than one window and clerk to serve patrons, thus avoiding annoyance over waiting an unreasonable amount of time for service. This room or building should be large enough to easily accommodate the staff with some

Fig 14,15/ Two examples of front-of-house structures, including lobby, entrance, lavatories, concessions, control booths, and lighting mounting positions. The top is from *Unto These Hills*, in Cherokee, NC; the bottom from *The Stephen Foster Story*, in Bardstown, KY.

additional space for storage of equipment and a safe for storage of receipts. Provision must be made for computers and a reliable internet connection since it is now standard practice to computerize the box office. The box office in some venues may also serve as a concierge-style information center.

Some theatre companies combine the box office with space for management personnel. The decision to include staff may depend on the location of the theatre in relation to the nearest town or city. With a remote venue, the management staff may prefer to be located in town rather than at the theatre. This issue should be considered in the planning of the whole operation as well as the performance facility.

Concessions

With many outdoor performance venues concessions can be quite elaborate. The Lake Tahoe Shakespeare Festival, for example, includes an extensive upscale food court, offering patrons gourmet entrees and snacks prepared by major restaurants in the area. Wine and beer are also served, creating a quite attractive reason to dine at the theatre before the performance. This creates a significant income stream for the company.

Most companies, however, provide more modest selections for their patrons. Even so, concessions may be as simple as the usual snacks offered at a movie theatre or the addition of a full meal before the show. Many companies do this not only for the income, but also to make attending the production more of an event. It is also worth noting that patrons coming from beyond the immediate area will appreciate not having to search for a restaurant in an unfamiliar area. This is especially attractive to families and large parties of patrons.

The extent of the concessions program should be determined in the planning process. The size of the concessions facility will depend first on the capacity of the theatre and second on the extent of service the company is willing to offer. But here, as with the box office, the concession service area must be large enough to serve large numbers of patrons in a short period of time since a significant portion of the concession business will occur at intermission. The same principle holds true if a meal is to be served prior to the performance. If that is the case, there must be tables and seating convenient to the concession stand.

Fig 16/ Intermission concessions, catering events, or full dinner service can be ways for theatres to increase both income and user experience. By developing an approach to food management early on, the facility can be designed to accommodate the technical and space requirements.

The concession room or building must be carefully planned. There are particular demands for cold and hot water, refrigeration, cooking and warming devices, basic storage and room for staff to prepare and serve concession offerings. Facility designers must also consult with local health officials to be sure that the facility meets all local and state health codes; that process should begin early in the planning stage. It is important to determine early whether food will be prepared on site or if the food will be cooked elsewhere and delivered to the site ready for sale and serving.

Gift Shop

While the establishment of a space for selling souvenirs and apparel is definitely a company's choice, there is no question that it can be a source of considerable income, especially for historical, religious and Shakespeare venues. Some theatre companies keep their gift shops open all day, picking up sales from visitors who visit the site or stop to buy tickets during the day. Planning this space depends on how extensive a selection of stock the company wishes to offer. Merchandise can range from tee shirts and other kinds of clothing to books and higher-end items. The key, however, is to place the gift shop in a convenient location, easily seen and found by patrons entering and leaving the theatre.

It may be possible to offer contracts to local merchants or food concessionaires to manage the concessions and gift shop. There is a distinct advantage in this practice since it relieves the theatre management from all of the details of preparing food, maintaining inventories of supplies and merchandise, and paying the staff to run these establishments. In such cases it is imperative to establish these relationships during the planning phase in order to assure that the facilities constructed for these operations are satisfactory to the concessionaires.

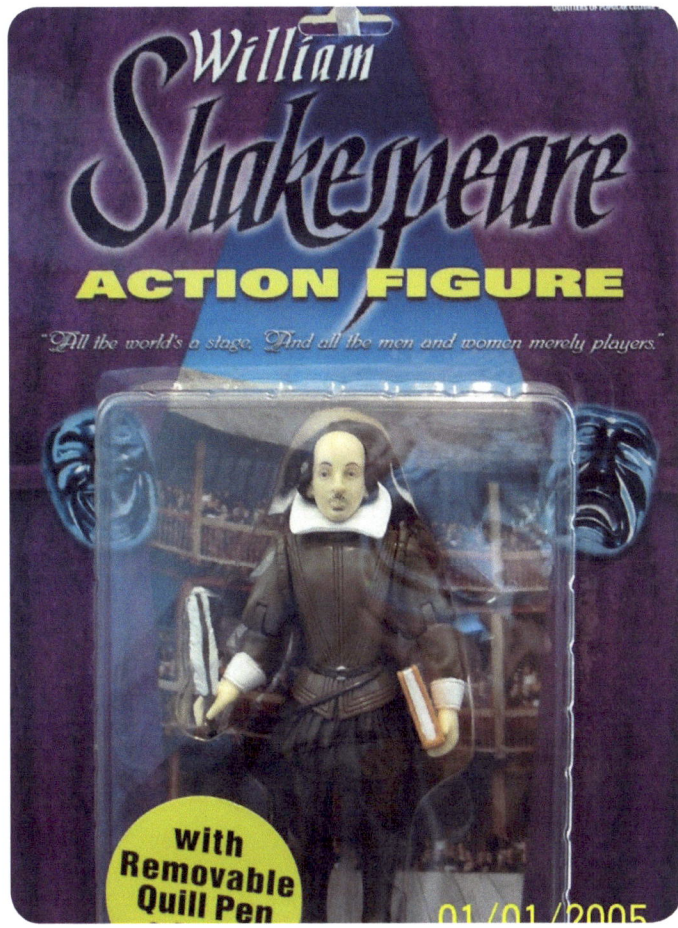

Fig 17/ To buy or not to buy?

Toilet Facilities

Providing toilet facilities for up to 1,000 patrons attending a theatrical performance can present several challenges for a company planning and building an outdoor theatre. Use of the facilities will be intensive for the brief period of the intermission, so the number of units must be sufficient to meet that demand. The number of toilets or urinals required will usually be established by local building codes, so these must be checked early in the planning stage. It has become standard in many communities, often by state law, to provide a set number of additional toilets for female patrons. Similarly, there are now state regulations regarding not only the number of toilets for disabled people, but the dimensions of these facilities as well. Based on the industry standard of one toilet or urinal for 30 patrons, the facility should provide approximately 34 toilet units in a 1,000-seat facility, approximately 12 units for men and 22 units for women.

Providing these accommodations is not a simple exercise. Added to the need for equipment and space is the issue of providing water and sewage control. If the venue is close to town or a reasonably well inhabited area, this may not be an issue since the company can utilize existing water and sewer lines. When the theatre is not served by public utilities, however, providing sufficient water can be an issue and sewage disposal will require a septic system. This can be costly and should be given careful and thorough consideration in the initial planning and choice of site.

Control Booth

For centuries the oversight and operations of a performance were managed entirely from backstage. By the middle of the 20th century, with advances in sound and light control, the operations center for theatrical performances shifted to the rear of the auditorium where the sound and lighting operators could better see and hear what was happening on the stage. It also became common for the stage manager, who is the true overseer of the production, to be located at the rear of the theatre where he or she can see everything happening on the stage. Assistant stage managers can manage the details of performance operations backstage.

This management location has become standard in outdoor venues as well. Ideally the control booth will be at the center rear of the amphitheatre and easily accessible. Many theatres place the booth a story or more above the last row of the audience. This has its advantages since the staff has a clear view of the whole stage and, in some cases, beyond. It can present a problem, however, in locations where local authorities are especially cautious about accessibility. It is important to remember that a person in a wheelchair could stage manage or operate a lighting or sound console.

If a production employs intricate sound, and especially individual microphones for the cast, the sound console will have to be either in a booth with a large open window or at a position in the audience space. It is necessary that the sound operator be able to hear what the audience is hearing in order to adjust sound levels appropriately. At the same time, it is essential that the sound console be protected from the weather.

The lighting console and stage manager's desk can be inside the booth and behind glass. There must be adequate desk space for all the consoles, monitors and computers that are now common for theatrical production. There should be sufficient outlets and connections for electrical service, intercommunication networks, speakers, microphones and control signals to all the dimmers controlling the lights. The extent of this equipment will be dictated by the intricacy of the performances for which the amphitheatre is planned.

Audience Seating and Sightlines

The design of the audience seating must take into consideration factors well beyond the number of seats and the sightlines to the performance areas. The following is a discussion of the issues that should be considered.

The number of seats in the amphitheatre auditorium is dependent on many factors. An auditorium that is rarely full might inadvertently suggest to the attendees that the presentations are not successful. An auditorium that has too few seats and is routinely full might result in lost potential box office revenue. Therefore, the determination of the optimum seat count is a critical decision.

Fig 18/ Shakespeare in Delaware Park is one of the largest free outdoor Shakespeare festivals in the country, located in Buffalo, NY. The festival attracts about 40,000 audience members each year. The facility was designed by Gary Casarella and is located in a public park designed by Frederick Law Olmsted.

In a recent audience survey conducted by an amphitheatre management team, comfortable seating was one of the top audience requests. It is difficult to provide seating in an outdoor venue that is equivalent to upholstered theatre seating that is available in most conventional indoor auditoriums. Audience seating in an outdoor environment can range from simple benches to portable lawn chair–type seats or to individual molded plastic, steel, or fiberglass seating units. Whichever type of seating is chosen, it is important to keep in mind comfort and durability. From the standpoint of custodial maintenance, riser-mounted seating facilitates easier floor cleaning than floor-mounted seating. While cup holders tend to connote movie theatre seating, performing arts managers are increasingly concluding that cup holders encourage the purchase of more concessions, which results in increased revenue.

The lifespan of the seating unit should be considered and well-documented in the bid documents and ensuing manufacturer's guarantee. While the plastic seat, for instance, might last for 100 years, the metal connectors might rust and deteriorate in a much shorter time frame if they are not a high-quality stainless steel.

The modern audience member perceives comfort based on the shape and 'give' of the seat bottom and back, the space between seats, the ergonomic design of the armrest, and the distance between seating rows. The demand for more seat comfort has resulted in seat widths that vary from 21 inches to 24 inches. Row-to-row distances are typically a minimum of 36 inches with 38 inch row-to-row dimensions becoming more typical. Seating layouts that employ aisles are more typical than the previously popular 'continental' style seating layouts with long, unbroken rows and more row-to-row width. The familiar ticket buyer call for 'Two on the aisle, please' continues to outweigh 'Excuse me, excuse me, excuse me.'

Sightlines from the seating area to the performance areas should be carefully considered and designed. The natural topography of the site is often a governing factor in the location and design of the amphitheatre. Conventional sightline design is based primarily on the concept of 'every other row seating,' which means that an individual two rows behind a more forward row can see over the head of the audience member two rows in front. 'Stadium seating' has become popular in the design of movie theatre seating layouts. In this arrangement, audience members can see over the heads of the people immediately in front of them. Stadium seating results in steep seating banks and a loss of the important feeling of communal experience. Stadium seating is difficult to construct through grading on typical sites due to the steepness of the required slopes. A site with a steep hillside to begin with can make stadium seating possible without the expense of constructed risers.

Auditorium design and seating layouts in the United States must conform to the requirements of the Americans with Disabilities Act (ADA), which decrees that handicapped audience members must have an equivalent choice of seats, seating locations and ticket prices as non-handicapped audience members. The ADA does not describe how to achieve these goals but that these goals are to be met. When possible, it is advisable to involve a local authority from the beginning of the design process to help to create the criteria and design goals for handicap seating layouts. The resulting seat layouts and auditorium designs should be reviewed by the local authority at key points in the design in order to verify that the design is indeed able to achieve the stated goals of the ADA legislation. Because ADA is enforced through discrimination suits, many times local building inspectors may overlook specific or specialized ADA clauses, but the facility owner and operator will still be liable. With today's litigious society, it is vitally important for the owner to take ADA and building code issues seriously, to hire licensed professionals and to manage the construction process cleanly with no shortcuts or omissions. A single ADA suit has the potential to cost millions of dollars and bankrupt the defendant organization, either through outright costs or crushing insurance after the fact.

If the seating area is totally or partially open to the weather, it is important to design the seating area so that rain water does not create pools under the feet of the audience members. In some amphitheatres, the floor area is dirt or sand, and the rain water quickly seeps away. If the floor area is concrete or some other hard material, it is critical that slopes and drains are provided to make sure that the rain water does not accumulate under the seating or on the aisles. A common design solution for this is a gentle slope on each level of seating, and trench drains incorporated into the amphitheater at intervals to avoid waterfalls in storm events.

Fig 19/ The 750-seat Minack Theatre (Cornish: *Gwaryjy Minack*) is an open amphitheatre, constructed on a granite outcrop jutting into the sea in Cornwall, UK. The location has been hosting theatre productions since 1929 and today about 80,000 patrons attend each year.

Stage and Backstage Requirements

Access to the Stage Area

The facility backstage must be accessible to trucks of all sizes, including emergency vehicles. This is especially true for a venue that plans to do different productions from one season to the next, or a venue that will serve as a booking house, bringing in different performance groups. Supplies of all kinds will be delivered to the stage area from time to time. Similarly, it is recommended that there be a parking area for the cast near the stage and dressing rooms. This can sometimes be problematic since vehicles should not be visible from the audience.

Dressing Rooms

Remarkable as it may be, theatres have been built without dressing rooms, at least until the first performance when someone realizes the mistake. Obviously these facilities are essential. Planning dressing rooms for outdoor performance creates a special problem in that there is not the protection from noise that is taken for granted with an indoor theatre. Thus the dressing room complex, usually needing to fulfill the needs of a large cast, has to be planned with careful consideration. The dressing rooms may be farther away from the stage than might be the case with an indoor theatre where doors and corridors can protect against undue noise.

The size and number of dressing rooms will be determined by the size of the onstage cast for a typical show and the types of productions that will be presented. If a theatre company or management plans to employ members of Actors' Equity, the actor's union, having separate small dressing rooms is a necessity. In addition, the union expects certain amenities to be in place as stated in the performers' contracts.

All dressing rooms should have convenient access to showers and toilets. Here again, the number of showers in each case will depend on the nature of the performance. In the case of historical plays that might include actors in group battle scenes or body paint, there may be need for a sizable gang shower. Acting outdoors in the heat and dirt makes the need of a shower after a performance attractive for all members of the company.

At least one shower facility for each sex must be equipped for disabled people. Similarly, there should be accessible toilet facilities. Smaller dressing rooms can be equipped for this use at the outset. It is also helpful, if budget permits, to have a separate toilet facility available outside the dressing rooms for the backstage crew, rather than requiring members of the crew to disturb the actors while they are preparing for the show. It is also often the case that technicians will be working during the day when the dressing rooms might be locked.

Depending on the location of the venue, standard air-conditioning may not be a desirable amenity for an outdoor venue. This is especially the case in locales where summer temperatures may be in the high nineties and above. Performers may have difficulty if they are preparing for a show in relatively cool comfort and then immediately go out into the heat to perform. Good ventilation should serve comfort needs if it is thoughtfully planned, but moderate air-conditioning is also a good possibility. Keeping the air-conditioning temperature just a few degrees cooler than the outside temperature will offer reasonable comfort without causing undue health problems. In addition, the drier air brought on with air-conditioning will help to maintain costumes and reduce mold buildup.

If no air-conditioning is opted for the dressing rooms, they should be well ventilated, but there should also be an air-conditioned space nearby should a performer become ill or suffer heat exhaustion. If planned from the beginning of the facility design, there are sustainable options for climate control, such as geothermal cooling, that can drastically reduce energy costs.

Each dressing room should offer counters with mirrors and lights for makeup. Individual vanity-type makeup stations are appropriate for the principal performers. For chorus members, it is not necessary to place vertically arranged lights between the mirrors. A row of lights above the mirrors will suffice. A shelf above the mirrors is a useful fixture for personal belongings. In the larger dressing rooms it is advisable to place counters and mirrors along each side of the room and costume racks down the middle. These racks should have a shelf at the bottom and another at the top for

Fig 20/ Well-planned back-of-house facilities contribute to economical and effective productions and positive performer-crew morale.

the various accessories that might be required. Ideally, racks should be on wheels so that costumes can be removed for laundering and repairs or, in a venue offering more than one production, changing the whole costume inventory to suit the different productions.

Another dressing room option allows for dressing in one room and a large, central makeup room for most of the cast. In current theatre practice many actors eschew makeup altogether or use it very sparingly, unless a special character makeup is required. Women, on the other hand, are more likely to want to apply a basic makeup and this should be accommodated.

The Green Room

Ever since the 17th century most theatres have provided a room where performers can assemble after getting dressed and applying their makeup. This is especially useful for actors who may have a scene and then have to wait for some time before another scene. The Green Room (there are many theories as to why it is called that) offers this option. With many outdoor venues this is simply a shed or covered space with seating rather than a specific room. But something like this facility should be a part of the backstage complex, and the option for offering drinks (at least water) and other refreshments there is worth serious consideration. Concessions providers may also serve food to the actors before the performances, and this can be considered during the planning stage. A designated smoking area is also a consideration and should be referenced as part of a smoking policy designed to protect health and safety.

Technical Spaces

Whatever the intended use for an outdoor amphitheatre one or more buildings are required to serve the technical needs of the venue. These needs begin with containment for electrical service for the theatre. This structure, or a large closet, may be backstage or as part of the front-of-house construction and is usually determined by the most practical relationship with the main electrical service to the facility. It is important that it be a sturdily built space that will always be dry and well ventilated. If the stage lighting dimmers are installed in the same room as the electrical service hardware (as is often the case), it is wise to provide air conditioning for the room. Locating the dimmer room in proximity to the majority of the lighting circuits and instrument locations can reduce the cost of conduit and wiring. LED-type lighting further reduces the need for conventional dimming equipment.

Beyond this essential space there can be a number of technical space choices depending upon the intended use for the amphitheatre. Some historical plays need a well-constructed and protected building to house firearms, ammunition, and explosive special effects materials. It is essential to work with local authorities as well as the Federal Bureau of Alcohol, Tobacco and Firearms to assure that all safety codes are taken into consideration. Typically, these storage areas need to be fireproof, windowless and auto-locking.

Another structure that will be required regardless of the use of the theatre is a workshop or scenic studio. Even if the scenery that will be used in the theatre is built elsewhere, there will always be a need for simple repairs and maintenance. On the other hand, if a production company intends to do a repertory of productions, with different shows from season to season (or even daily or weekly), it might be desirable to have a fairly extensive scenic studio. This can be determined in the overall planning for the venue.

While the scenic studio can accommodate a variety of functions, it is wise to have a separate facility for the storage and maintenance of properties. A small, secure building for this purpose will assure good organization of all the small items that are necessary for performances. Placing such a building at each side of the stage assures easy access and better organization from one performance to the next.

Costumes have another set of requirements, even if there is only the need to maintain and repair the clothing worn by the actors. Essential in this case is the appropriate

Fig 21/ While all the possible uses of the facility cannot be accounted for in the design and planning process, the key technical needs, such as loading, striking, fabrication, costume making, lighting, sound, and rehearsal space, will make the facility a more efficient venue.

number of washers and dryers to accommodate the number of costumes that need to be processed. It is often necessary to do laundry every night during a hot summer. Theatre companies employing large casts should consider providing industrial-size laundry equipment. There must also be adequate space for working on the costumes in a comfortable, air-conditioned and well-lit environment.

These are the basic support structures that will be required. Many of the functions can be served in one building, but care must be taken to assure that there is no conflict in operations. For example, a scenic studio cannot be too close to the costume studio, partly to avoid the nuisance of noise from scenery construction but also to prevent construction dirt and debris from damaging costumes.

The Crossover

No matter what form the backstage area takes—roofed or open to the sky—actors and technicians need to go from one side of the stage to the other undetected by the audience. This is usually accomplished using scenic elements or other built structure to mask a backstage crossover, but at least one amphitheatre (Val Chatel, MN) accomplished it with a tunnel that passed under the audience. The drama *Conquistador* in Hot Springs, AR, used a deep trench behind the stage that allowed riders on horseback to pass from one side of the stage to the other. No matter what the intended use of the theatre, this is important to include in the planning process, and the solution should consider the aesthetics of the venue and its intended purpose.

Fig 22/ Fire, water and horses are all easily possible for outdoor productions, but the facility should be designed to enable their anticipated use, including stables, safe pyrotechnical support areas, and crossovers. A Serenbe Playhouse production.

The Stage

The stage space within which performances will take place obviously will vary considerably depending on the kinds of entertainment being offered, and whether the stage will be roofed or not. Details of the stage will be noted below and in other portions of this document. The primary concern in the planning stage is the determination of an appropriate size for the stage. Historical plays that involve many scenes and a broad scope, including battle scenes, dances, and casts of 50 or more on the stage at a time will usually require a playing area of 60' or more in width. A common rule of thumb for the depth of the stage is somewhere from 30' to 40', though this is again determined by the intended use. A company intending to present plays or musicals with smaller casts may easily diminish the fundamental width of the playing area. Most Broadway plays and musicals perform on stages with 36' to 40' proscenium arches so that could easily apply in this instance. The stage width may also be affected by the width of the seating in the amphitheatre. The plans and elevations included in this report are based on a seat count of 1,000. The widths noted above would be quite appropriate for that level of seating.

That is not the total width of the stage space, of course. Off-stage space is needed at each side and the amount will be determined by the intended use for the facility. If, for instance, the company plans to produce several plays in one season or in weekly or daily rotation, the extra off-stage space will be necessary.

Whether or not there is a roof over the stage will have a considerable impact on the space under that roof, but for most of the venues considered in this document a roof over the stage is highly desirable. This is an important consideration in planning the theatre because of the cost of the structure, but the advantages of a roof in all but the site-specific venues are considerable. They include protection from the weather for musical groups as well as actors, protection for the scenery, and a much better option for stage lighting positions than an open-to-the-sky stage. Examples of covered stages are found in Chapter 5 of this report.

The structure that supports the roof over the stage will allow some modest stage rigging that will be helpful with specific productions. The roof structure also permits the inclusion of catwalks so that technicians can easily and safely move about above the stage. The complexity above the stage does not need to be echoed over the off-stage spaces, and it is even possible that very little of the off-stage area will be covered. While a fully rigged stagehouse above the stage is an option, it is doubtful that such an element, with its resulting costs, would be necessary or cost-effective.

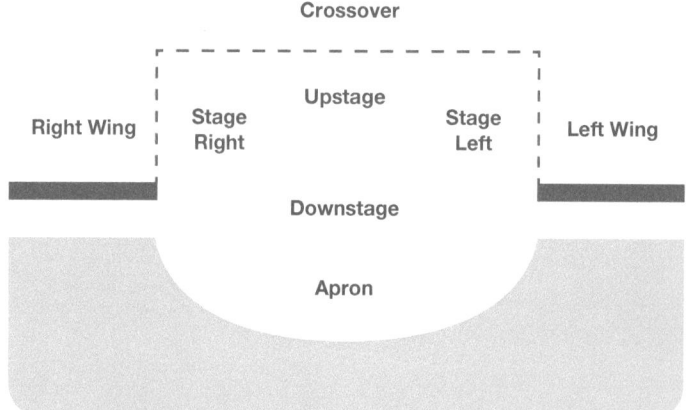

Fig 23/ Diagram of a stage.

Stage Floor

Decisions on what surface is best for outdoor stages have varied according to the type of production offered in a given venue. The outdoor historical theatres for many years preferred a fairly deep sand floor for a variety of reasons. Often sand was chosen because it suited the natural look while also allowing comfort for the actors indulging in battle scenes. But as theatres were built for shows that did not have that need, other solutions were developed. In some instances the choice was obvious: concrete. This is the most durable solution but not always the best choice if a company is doing shows that include a fair amount of dancing. Concrete is hard on the feet and may cause painful shin splints. Dancing on concrete should be strictly avoided.

Some theatres have tried asphalt as a stage floor, but that is not ideal when the black surface holds the heat of the day into the performance hours. Another choice is a structural clay, similar to tennis court material, that has the advantage of being able to take color that makes it look more natural. Wood is always an option, but any sort of standard wood flooring may wear badly under the hot sun and frequent rains. Some more weather-resistant woods include ipe, black locust, redwood, and red cedar. These woods are highly resistant to rot, damage from rain and termites, and are low-splinter timber. When wood is used as a stage surface, it is important that the wood be of an edge-grain cut, to reduce the possibility of dangerous splintering.

The choice of floor surface obviously depends on budget and intended use, and it is made much simpler if the stage is to be roofed. Even in that case care should be taken in the choice of materials since blown rain may cause damage. In the latter third of the 20th century a new choice appeared: a composite material used for running tracks and playgrounds. There are now several manufacturers of this material, commonly called 'safety surface'. Safety surface is a permanent surface and is typically laid and glued on a concrete base. (Safety surface was applied at *The Stephen Foster Story* and is still holding up well.) Safety surface comes in a variety of colors suitable to the natural environment of the area or, if the theatre is intended for multiple production use, a straightforward black. Not only is safety surface durable, but it offers a much more forgiving surface for actors and dancers.

Fig 24/ Outdoor constructed stages, whether made of concrete and intended to last 30 years, or plywood and intended to last the season, need to be designed to accommodate weather and slip hazards. Utah Shakespeare Festival, *Richard III*.

Fig 25/ Turf is best for low-use areas or short productions—the rugged use required for summer stock or permanent facilities will destroy turf. Nevertheless, with adequate rest time, turf can be an attractive and soft stage surface. Utah Shakespeare Festival, *The Tempest*.

Fig 26/ Sand has been used for many historical dramas, and while cheap and 'soft,' sand is a problematic surface for effective dance and stage combat action as well as limiting the ability to change scenery efficiently with rolling platforms. *The Lost Colony*, Roanoke Island, NC.

Lighting Positions

Even though many outdoor performances begin in daylight or twilight, there is almost no feature among the equipment for a theatre that is more important than the lighting. Placement of the stage lights can become a serious issue with outdoor theatres, but the need for total concealment has diminished in recent years as audiences have become more accustomed to seeing the stage lighting fixtures in contemporary production. This is especially true with popular music concerts. Some directors and designers, however, prefer to conceal the lighting as much as possible.

Placement of lighting fixtures on lighting towers, under the roof of the pavilion at the rear of the theatre or over a portion of the audience are all viable options. If the venue is especially large and therefore the lighting instruments have an especially long throw to the stage, placing lights on the pavilion may be impractical and expensive. In that case front-of-house lighting can be accomplished with light towers placed at each side of the seating area approximately halfway back from the front of the stage. These locations are optimum with a theatre of 1,000 seats or fewer, making the throw to the stage at that distance feasible with economically priced fixtures. Even with the pavilion option it may be desirable to erect towers at each side of the amphitheatre for lights that add a dimension to the performers that is highly desirable. Lighting angles from the lighting position to the stage must be carefully considered. Angles that are too low should be avoided as primary lighting positions.

Roofed stages allow for lighting options similar and equal to those in an indoor theatre. Even though there may be many fixtures aimed at the stage from the rear of the theatre there is still need for lights above and/or at the sides of the stage in order to effectively light the performers. Accommodations must therefore be made for hanging and adjusting lights as needed. (Specifics about lighting instrumentation are addressed in Chapter 4.)

No matter where the lighting fixtures are placed, depending on the choice of theatre design, technicians will have to gain access to the lights for focusing and general maintenance. In a roofed facility catwalks can provide access to the majority of the lights. If lights are a part of the pavilion or on

Fig 27/ Light towers. American Players Theatre, Spring Green, WI.

towers at the sides of the amphitheatre access can be more difficult. By planning for access in advance, the facility will be much safer, and this is decidedly an issue, given current state and federal laws. Establishing the proper devices and safety aids at the beginning can assure the safest possible work site. Safety for the audience, performers and technical staff is paramount in the design and the operation of the facility. Reducing the need for complex rigging and numbers of lights that require five-point safety harnesses to access can also dramatically reduce the expense of managing and adjusting this equipment.

Whether lights are protected by a roof or not, care must be taken to protect the wiring and circuitry from water. The fixtures themselves are not usually an issue today because they are no longer made of steel (subject to rust) as was the case for many years. Plastic and aluminum are the usual materials, except for some small parts inside the instruments, from which lights are now made and they are not negatively affected by water. Even the lenses are now made of plastic rather than glass, thus avoiding the old problem of breakage from being struck by cold rain. Wiring should be housed in code-required conduit to protect it from the elements as well as from hungry squirrels and other animals looking for food during the off-season. Plugging boxes should be weather-proof, regardless of whether they are protected from the rain.

These conditions simply argue that special care must be taken in planning for the lighting system that will be created for any outdoor theatre. There will be considerable wiring that begins with simply providing electricity, but contemporary lighting may also call for specific low-voltage control wiring, should any remote control devices (color changers, movable spotlights, etc.) be a part of the design. However, progress is being made toward wireless remote control and that may well be an option worth exploring as plans develop. The ongoing advances in the design of LED-based performance lighting instruments make LED instruments increasingly more viable for the outdoor venue application with remarkable energy savings and extended lifespan in comparison to traditional lighting.

Special Options

Depending on the intended use of the venue, there may be need to consider various options for special effects and particular production needs. For example, running water or a pond might be good features, or the use of fireworks could be an option. In the future, more and more effects of all kinds might become available for use outdoors, some of them especially attractive because they cannot be used indoors. Projected effects may become a compelling addition to the design of a production. While some of these issues might not be predictable at the time the building is being designed, some thought should be given to all possibilities to determine whether provisions should be made for them in the physical construction. These issues alone may be part of the thought process to determine whether or not a stage and amphitheatre should be roofed. Only careful thought about the ultimate uses of the venue can fully determine what these options might demand and whether or not they can be included in the initial planning for the facility.

Two structural features are worth considering in the planning stages. One of these is an orchestra pit. While many productions now use recorded music in support of musical theatre performance, some theatres may prefer to use live accompaniment. In the outdoor venue this can be a difficult problem in that the orchestra should not be caught in the pit by a shower. Some companies have solved this issue by putting the orchestra to one side or even behind the performers with video screens showing the conductor visible to the actors. There is no question that there are serious issues of cost and use related to the inclusion of a pit in the planning of the theatre. Relatively few outdoor venues have true orchestra pits.

Another space that many theatres find desirable is a rehearsal hall. This can be a simple structure that is as large as the playing space of the stage plus a few additional square feet for the cast and staff to work comfortably. The building should be air-conditioned and must also include toilets unless they are readily accessible nearby. Often the rehearsal hall is close enough to the dressing rooms for those toilets to be available. Locating a building for this purpose that is also easily accessed by the audience can be very useful as a gathering place for public occasions, cast parties and even small workshop productions. During the off-season this structure also can be a valuable rental facility or can function as a storage space.

Fig 28/ An orchestra pit can both provide a space to accommodate live music performance and also be a creative staging opportunity.

Chapter 4

Performance Equipment

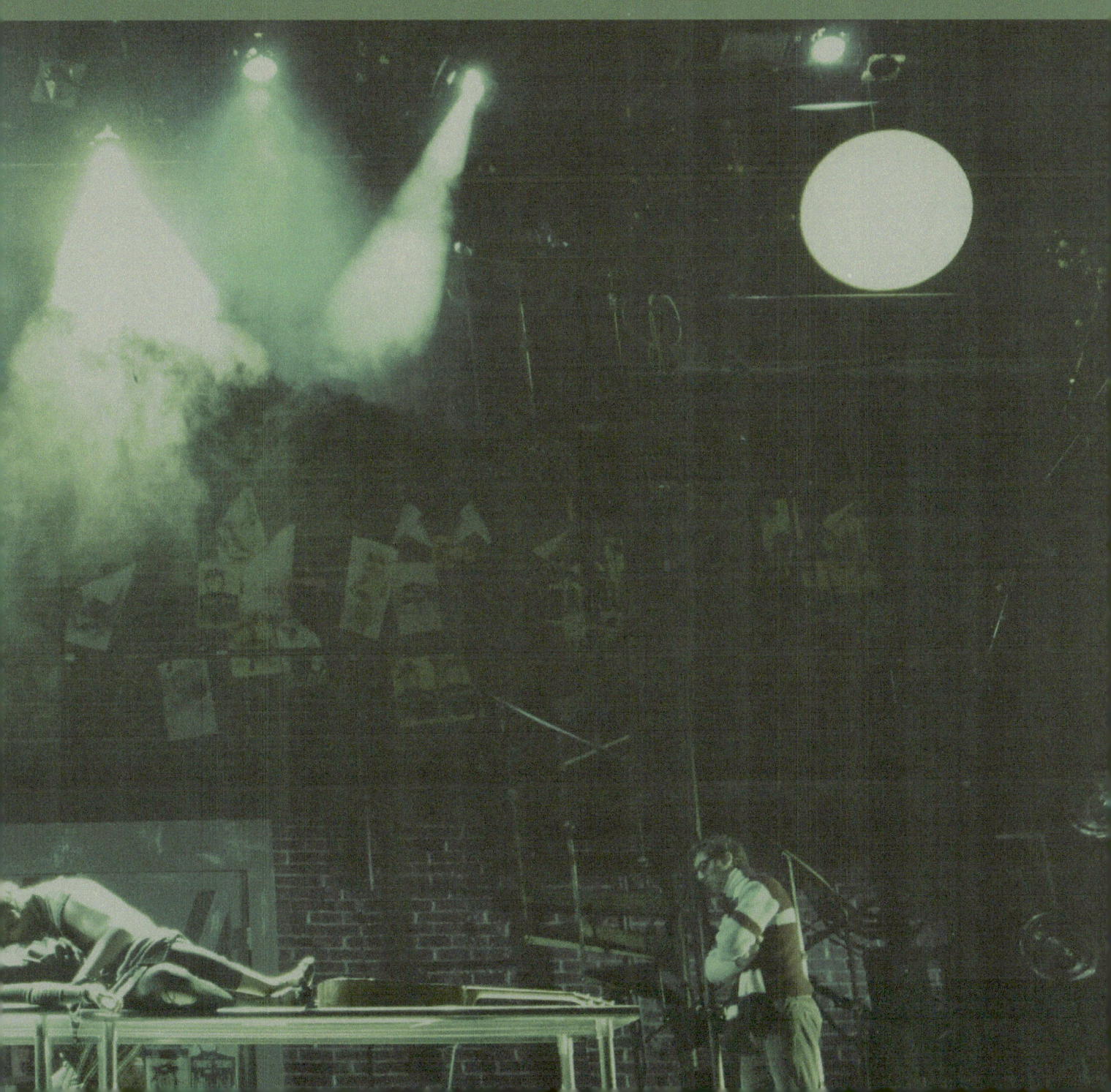

The Performance Equipment

The following is a description of the basic performance equipment systems that are customarily used in outdoor production facilities, comments on how to procure this equipment, and recommendations for the maintenance and storage of the equipment.

Lighting

Performance lighting systems are composed of three primary elements: lighting fixtures, dimming and control systems and circuit distribution devices. Most facilities maintain a variety of instrument types to provide various lighting functions and effects. Incandescent light sources have been the mainstay for theatrical lighting for nearly 100 years, requiring theatre companies to maintain an inventory of light bulbs or 'lamps' of various types and wattages in order to quickly replace burn-outs.

In recent years a new lamp, based on LED technology, has become an acceptable alternative for many theatrical applications; fixtures utilizing these lamps are becoming more available and are replacing existing incandescent fixtures. The choice of all LED units or a mix of LED and incandescent fixtures must be considered as the technology becomes more common. There is no question that LED lamps are far more efficient in that they will burn for ten or more years. In addition, the units contain an inherent dimming function as well as a virtually unlimited selection of colors.

The most significant downside to the use of LED-based lighting equipment is that the instruments cost approximately three to four times as much as a conventional incandescent instrument. The cost of these LED fixtures, however, will decrease as demand for these instruments increases. LED light sources have a published lifespan of approximately 20,000 hours. Reduced energy consumption and no longer having to maintain an inventory of replacement lamps help to balance the difference in cost of LED versus incandescent. In general, an incandescent lamp-based performance lighting system is not energy efficient and requires the frequent replacement of lamps, a dimmer bank installation, disposable 'gel' media to provide various colors, and more electrical infrastructure.

Fig 29/ LED alternatives to traditional theatre lights, such as this PARcan alternative, have huge energy savings and life span, offsetting initial higher cost. As the technology has improved the former 'cold' light stereotype has been replaced with a wide range of color rendering.

The trade-off is between a higher cost for the LED lighting units and a reduced cost for the electrical system. While the initial investment may be greater, the return in the long run is considerable not just in cost but in convenience. With these considerations, it is possible that a theatre might choose to start with a hybrid system employing both LED and incandescent lighting fixtures. The decision in this regard will have a major impact on the choices for dimming and control equipment as well as circuit distribution. A knowledgeable lighting designer or consultant should be engaged to assist in this decision.

Lighting designers are becoming increasingly more creative and demanding in terms of lighting outdoor productions. It is important in the design or renovation of an amphitheatre to consider how best to provide a range of lighting positions. These can include traditional front-of-house lighting from roof locations and side lighting towers, to proscenium wall side lighting and other unique positions. Depending on the type of productions anticipated for the amphitheatre facility, motorized 'intelligent' lights or moving lights, as well as color changers, might be required or desired by the lighting designers. It is important to locate these units so that they are less susceptible to damage from rain, dust and salt.

In this era of sustainability, owners and facility designers may find themselves in the middle of the debate between the 'traditionalists' who are most comfortable with conventional incandescent lighting equipment and the 'futurists' who have confidence in the ability of the new LED-based lighting devices. Until this debate is settled, the third alternative is to embrace both technologies and to provide sufficient infrastructure to allow for both to be used successfully.

Sound and Communication

Sound devices have been used as an element of outdoor production at least since the advent of the Greek theatre when megaphones were built into the headdresses of the major performers. Modern audiences have an increasing expectation of the sound that they perceive during a performance. The modern ear wants more information, both louder and clearer. Sound systems are used in many cases to amplify voices, instruments, sound effects, public address announcements, and for hearing-assist systems required by the ADA.

Outdoor performance facilities have the added challenge of not having complete control over the acoustical environment. Sound from the natural environment can include wind, water, insects and thunder. Sound from the manmade environment can include traffic noise as well as distracting noise of trains, airplanes, sirens and mechanical systems. When selecting a site for a new theatre, the level of acoustic interference from any or all of these sources is an important consideration. Although the perfectly quiet environment will probably never be possible, that aspect of a site should at least be evaluated.

Sound systems have become essential elements of almost all performance facilities. Unlike performance lighting systems that are often purchased from a single provider, sound systems are typically created from components that are assembled from a variety of manufacturers, based on the design requirements that have been prescribed by the system designer. This mix-and-match approach is standard for the industry. Sound system equipment can cost more than any of the other performance systems categories and is subject to a shorter life span as well. This requires a more frequent financial investment to keep the system in optimum performance condition.

Designers of an outdoor theatre facility need to provide optimum locations for the placement of sound system speakers. The trend toward partially covered and fully covered stages and auditoriums is driven to an extent by the enhanced ability to improve the quality of the audience's experience via the sound environment. Sound system speakers are often positioned at the sides of the proscenium opening and, if feasible, in a high center location. As with the performance lighting instruments, sound equipment will last longer and perform better if protected as much as is practical from the outdoor environment.

Other elements of the performance sound system include the production intercom system that connects the various technical and production staff; the 'show relay' system that supplies sound from the stage to areas including the control booth, follow-spot platforms, dressing rooms, green room, rehearsal room, and various public areas in the front-of-house; the ADA-mandated hearing-assist system; and any projection and video monitor equipment that might be provided.

Fig 30/ Sound equipment under shelter.

Rigging

A roof over the stage of an outdoor performance facility serves several functions. If designed properly, the roof will protect the performers and their costumes, musical instruments, scenery and props from inclement weather. The roof can be designed to enhance the movement of acoustical energy between the stage and the audience seating area and to partially buffer the stage from outside noise. The roof structure also allows for the installation of a performance rigging system. The types of performance rigging systems that could be installed include:

- A system of static pipe battens hung on rigging cable or chain from the roof and accessed from the stage floor by ladder, scaffold or personnel lift.
- A conventional manually operated counterweight rigging installation.
- A system of motorized pipe battens.
- A system of adjustable pipe battens and spot-line sets that use conventional chain-motor technology.

The choice of one of these systems, or a combination of two or more of the above, is dependent on the type of productions to be presented, the frequency of both repeating and changing presentations, the cost of the installation, the skill and experience of the production staff, the design of the facility, and the safety of the performers and production staff. Safety is of paramount importance.

Static pipe battens might be sufficient for supporting performance lighting and basic masking draperies, but they do not provide for the vertical manipulation of scenic and drapery elements. For outdoor theatres in humid or dusty climates, the more 'moving pieces' (such as pulleys and counterweights) used, the more important regular greasing and maintenance of these systems will be for both safety and guaranteed performance. The conventional manually operated counterweight rigging system has more structural and operational requirements and tends to be more appropriate for a full-height stagehouse of at least 50'.

Although motorized rigging equipment is perhaps the most desirable choice for the rigging installation, the cost and the relatively low annual usage in a seasonal facility suggests that this type of rigging might not be cost-effective. Conventional chain-motor rigging provides flexibility for where and how to position rigging battens and spot-lines. The equipment is used widely in rock-and-roll touring installations. It is portable, can be stored easily when not in use, and can potentially be rented or leased if purchase is a less desirable option.

The preferred solution, again, depends on the number and type of productions that will be presented in the facility, the technical abilities of the production staff, the available budget, and the design of the facility.

Fig 31/ In open conditions, such as the Kingsmen Shakespeare Company's performances in Kingsmen Park, trusses can be erected to provide the structure for the rigging. Kingsmen Shakespeare Company, Thousand Oaks, CA.

Fig 32/ A partial or full roof can provide ample space for rigging, lighting positions, and sound equipment, as seen here at the Miller Outdoor Theatre, Houston, TX.

Stage Draperies

If the amphitheatre stage is to be used for a variety of performance types and does not have a permanently installed scenic background, then a set of stage masking curtains and 'back cloths' will be useful for creating a traditional masked stage when required. The use of these curtains is further dependent on the ability to suspend them from rigging battens or other structural elements. If the stage does not have a roof structure, then it is probable that these curtains would not be necessary, unless there is a means for suspending them via floor-supported devices. In some cases, these masking curtains might be achieved in the form of framed 'flats,' which are more resistant to sudden or persistent wind conditions.

Since the stage and auditorium are not enclosed within a conventional building, the curtain material is subject to the changing outside environment, whether or not there is a partial or full roof system over the stage and auditorium. To deal with the impact of the varying humidity, it is recommended that the curtains be made from polyester fabric rather than from organic cotton material. The polyester is more resilient and will last longer in this semi-outdoor environment. Back cloths, which include the 'cyclorama' curtain and 'scrim' curtains, are available in a variety of materials.

Controlled storage of these curtains during the performance season and especially during the 'off' season should be carefully provided so that the fabric is protected from mildew, pests, and damage to the surfaces and color.

Fig 33, 34/ Curtains and back cloths are useful for facilities hosting a range of events, such as the Jay Pritzker Pavilion in Chicago's Millennium Park, designed by Frank Gehry.

Design and Procurement

Portions of the performance equipment systems, such as permanent wiring, that are described above should be provided and installed under the supervision of the general contractor (GC) or construction manager (CM), but the majority of this equipment can be purchased in a timely manner by the client or owner of the amphitheatre facility. When the owner purchases the miscellaneous equipment, often referred to as 'fixtures, furnishings and equipment' (FF&E) directly, the cost will not be increased by the markup added by the GC or CM, thus saving money for the owner. Items that can be purchased directly by the owner include such equipment as the performance lighting instruments, portable stage cable, the control console, portable components of the sound and communications systems, the entirety of the stage drapery system including curtain tracks, and other such equipment.

The elements that should be installed within the construction contract are portions of the performance lighting system and the sound and communications systems that require normal electrical voltage as well as electrical power supplies, junction boxes, back boxes and conduit. Portions of the stage rigging system may best be provided and installed within the construction contract, depending on the choice of rigging equipment, as equipment that is attached to the structure is best installed by the contractor. An important benefit of contractor installation is the additional warranty and liability protection that this can provide.

The role of a contracted theatre consultant during design and construction includes assistance with the selection and acquisition of the performance equipment systems. The theatre consultant will begin by gaining an understanding of what the owner intends for the facility to do. Then the consultant will prepare a detailed list of equipment, including quantities and projected costs. When the owner has reviewed and approved these recommendations, the consultant will then begin the process of coordinating the equipment with the structural and electrical engineers, under the guidance of the architect. The theatre consultant will produce drawings and specifications for the performance equipment prior to the completion of the facility design, and will assist the owner with the determination of how best to acquire the performance equipment.

Depending on the frequency of use, the length of the production season, the capability of the technical staff, and the overall economics, the option of renting or leasing the portable components of the performance equipment systems should be considered. Renting the equipment rather than purchasing it may make economic sense in some instances.

Off-Season Storage

If the owner chooses to purchase the equipment rather than to rent or lease it, the equipment must be stored properly so that it is safe and protected from the elements during the off-season. For this reason, the theatre's architectural program should include adequate storage space. Depending on what is to be stored during the off-season, that space may need to include fire protection (sprinklers) and have humidity and/or climate control systems to protect from mildew, rot and corrosion. Fabric storage in particular can attract rodents and insects. Designing for a pest-free environment can affect the details of the architecture, from increasing the extent of flashing to bulking up vents and soffit materials.

Fig 35 / In order to reuse costumes, props, and sets, storage space should be protected from pests, fire, humidity, sunlight, and vandalism.

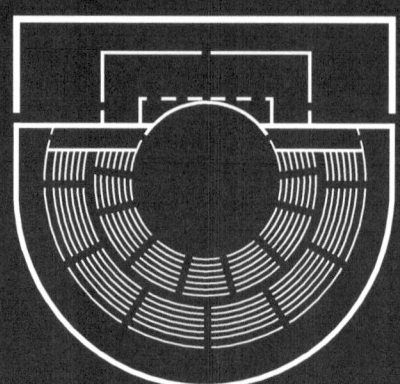

Chapter 5

Types of Outdoor Theatres

Five Models

After much discussion, the research team for this study has identified five distinct models of outdoor theatre facilities, which are described in the following sections. Like all categorizations, this one is imperfect and, in fact, the last two might more accurately be referred to as collections rather than models. Nevertheless, we believe that this fairly represents the variety of theatres in existence today in a way that should be helpful to organizations planning to renovate existing theatres or build new theatres in the future.

 **Open Stage with Open Amphitheatre**

 **Roofed Stage with Open Amphitheatre**

 **Roofed Stage and Amphitheatre**

 **Temporary Theatres**

 **Hybrid Theatres**

Model #1: Open Stage with Open Amphitheatre

Amphitheatron (ἀμφιθέατρον) is the ancient Greek word describing a semi-circular place for viewing performances. Today the amphitheatre is still the most familiar type of outdoor theatre structure. The Greek theatres were sited on a hillside, with stone risers or stairs built into the hill for access and seating. The slope of seating area provided good sightlines to the ground-level stage area below, and the bowl shape of the amphitheatre enhanced the acoustic properties of the performance. A façade was located at the rear of the stage area to assist in reflecting sound, provide a crossover for the actors, and hide the stage equipment and actor dressing areas. Performances took place during daylight hours.

The amphitheatre continued to evolve in ancient Rome with several architectural additions:

- A raised stage replaced the ground-level performance area.
- The façade at the rear of the stage became more elaborate and was pierced with doors and windows to provide entrances and balcony appearances.
- The semi-circular seating area was constructed rather than relying on a natural hill for its slope.
- All the theatre elements were integrated into a single connected structure. Later, during the Renaissance, the earliest indoor theatres were created by adding a roof to this Roman model and weatherproofing it.

Many outdoor theatres throughout the world today continue to follow the Greco-Roman model with modern additions to address the requirements of contemporary audiences and theatre technology. As shown in our amphitheatre drawings in this document and described in Chapter 2, a pavilion at the top of the theatre serves to welcome and shelter the audience as well as housing toilets, management and ticket offices, concessions, front lighting of the stage, and technical control booths. Lighting towers are frequently added on either side of the seating area to provide additional locations for lighting instruments. The stage may be packed soil or sand, or it may be built up as in the Roman model. Backstage spaces with loading zones, dressing rooms, shops, rehearsal and storage areas are added and can be simple or complex, depending on the needs of the theatre. Many modern amphitheatres, like their ancient counterparts, are often sited on a natural slope, while others construct the seating area with the necessary angle for sightlines.

An open amphitheatre is a term applied to an amphitheatre without a roof structure. The cost of building an open amphitheatre is almost always less than any other type of permanent outdoor theatre simply because there is less to build and maintain. Without protection from the elements, however, events in an open amphitheatre are much more prone to cancellation because of weather, and the seasonal window in which events can be produced or presented tends to be smaller.

Fig 36 / Open Stage with Open Amphitheatre Plan Legend:

1. Pavilion
2. Box Office
3. Concessions
4. Office
5. Storage
6. Men
7. Women
8. Electrical
9. Control Booth
10. Light/Sound Locks
11. Amphitheatre—1,000 Seats
12. Cross Aisle—ADA Access
13. Light Towers
14. Main Stage
15. Side Stage
16. Stage Entries
17. Crossover

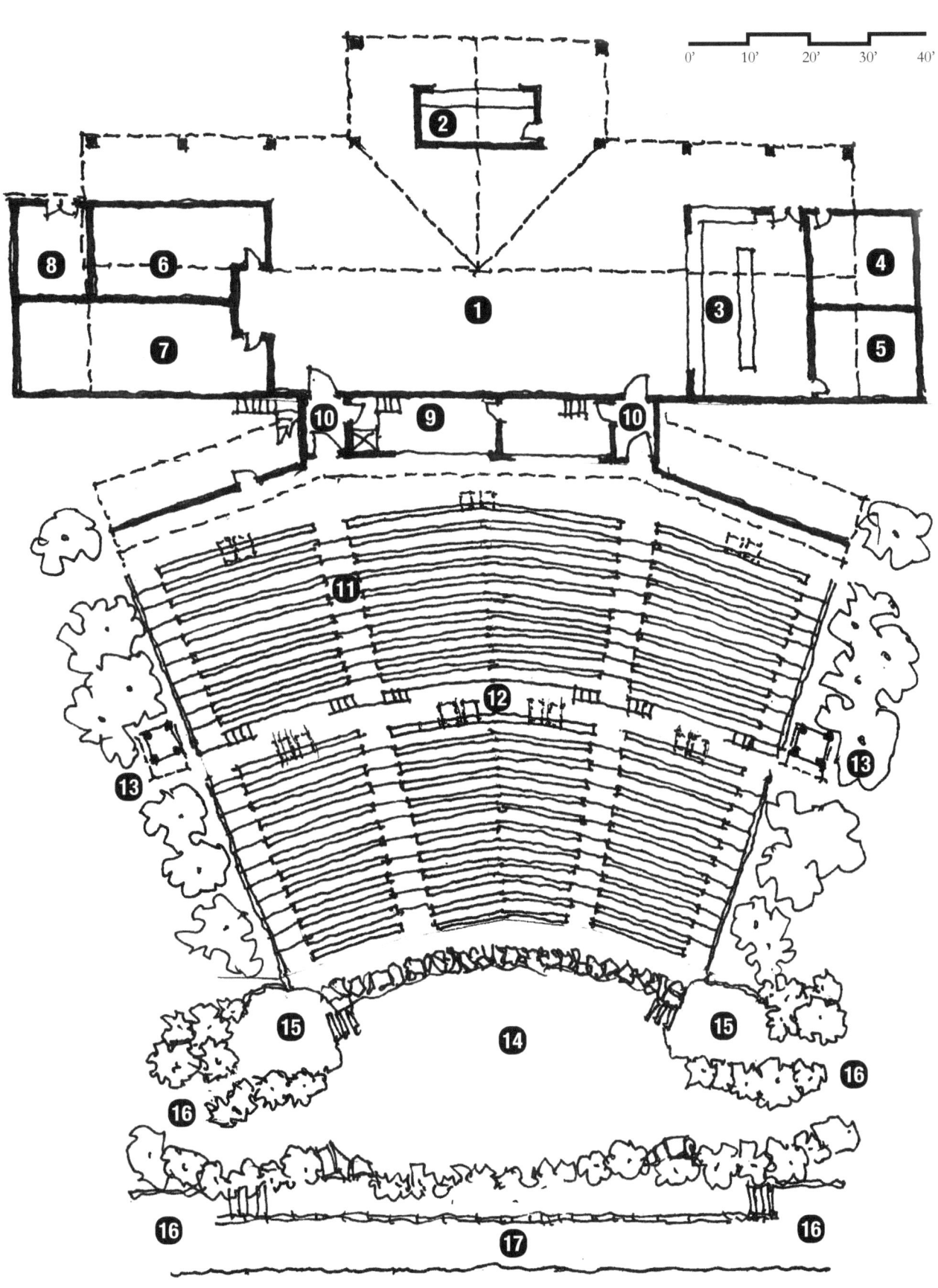

Depending on the climate of a particular location, an open amphitheatre may not be an effective venue for presenting a range of performance types: this is particularly true for musical events that constitute the majority of available touring programs. There are two basic programming patterns for open amphitheatres:

1. Repeated performances of one or two 'signature' productions with a main production that is repeated every year. This is typically the case with historical dramas and religious pageants, a number of which have performed for well over 50 years.

2. A variety of performances that are either produced in a summer stock format or as a mix of produced or presented events.

An amphitheatre that produces signature attractions has typically been designed and built with a particular story in mind. It is often in a location that is related to the theme of the main play, such as the site where the historical event depicted actually took place. These productions tend to be substantial in terms of scenery, costumes and lighting and often utilize large numbers of performers, either paid or volunteer. Because the main attraction plays for all or the

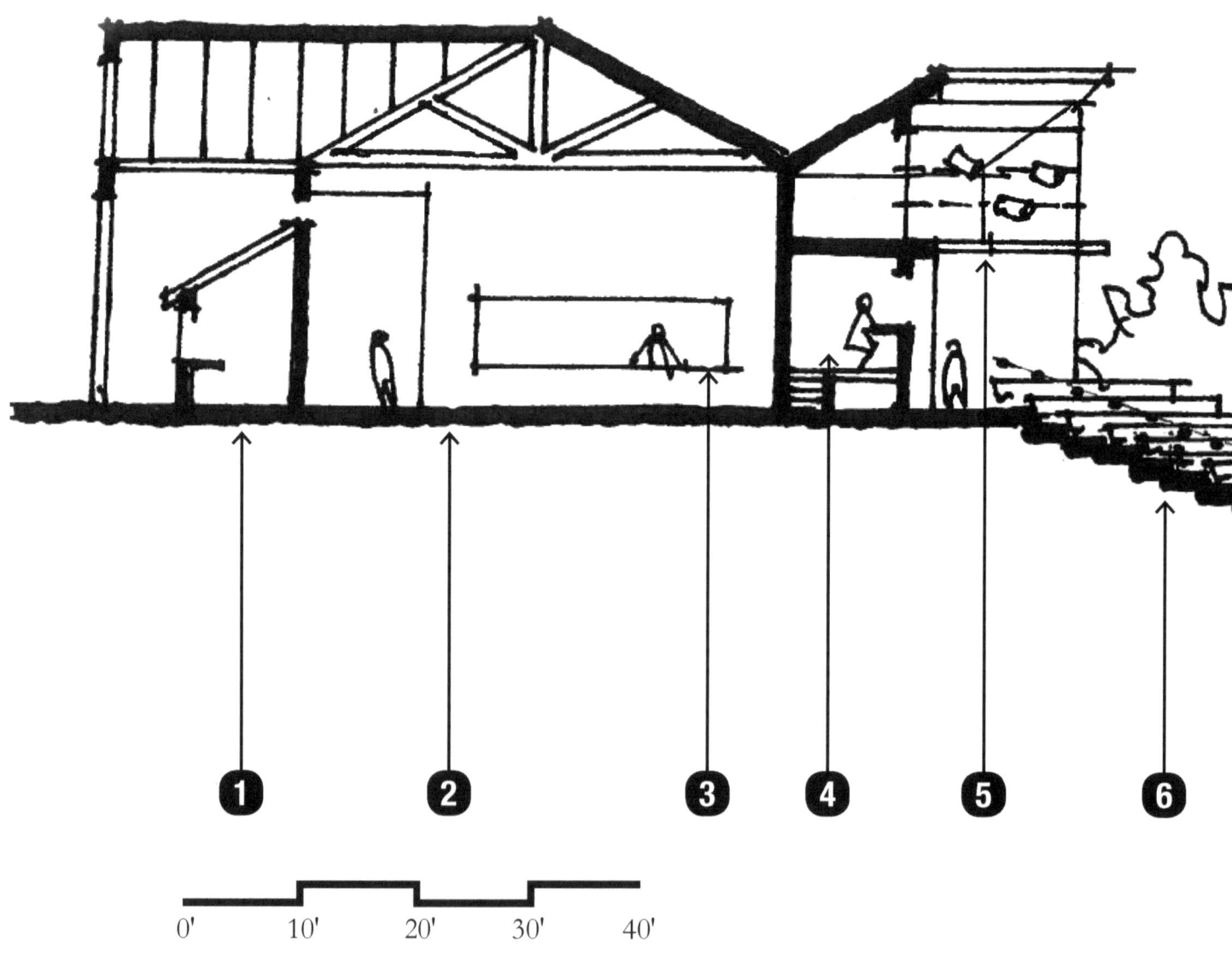

major part of the season year after year, the production tends to grow and become more elaborate over time as successive artistic directors and designers make their contribution to its traditions. There is little need to 'clear the stage' to make room for other productions and, if a different show is occasionally scheduled, it often performs with the main production's setting as a backdrop. With a historical or religious theme, the natural artistic impulse is to create an illusion of historical authenticity, so scenery and costumes tend to be realistic rather than stylized.

Fig 37 / Open Stage with Open Amphitheatre Section Legend:

1. Box Office
2. Pavilion
3. Concessions
4. Control Booth
5. Lighting Deck
6. Amphitheatre—1,000 Seats
7. Cross Aisle—ADA Access
8. Light Towers
9. Main Stage
10. Side Stage
11. Crossover

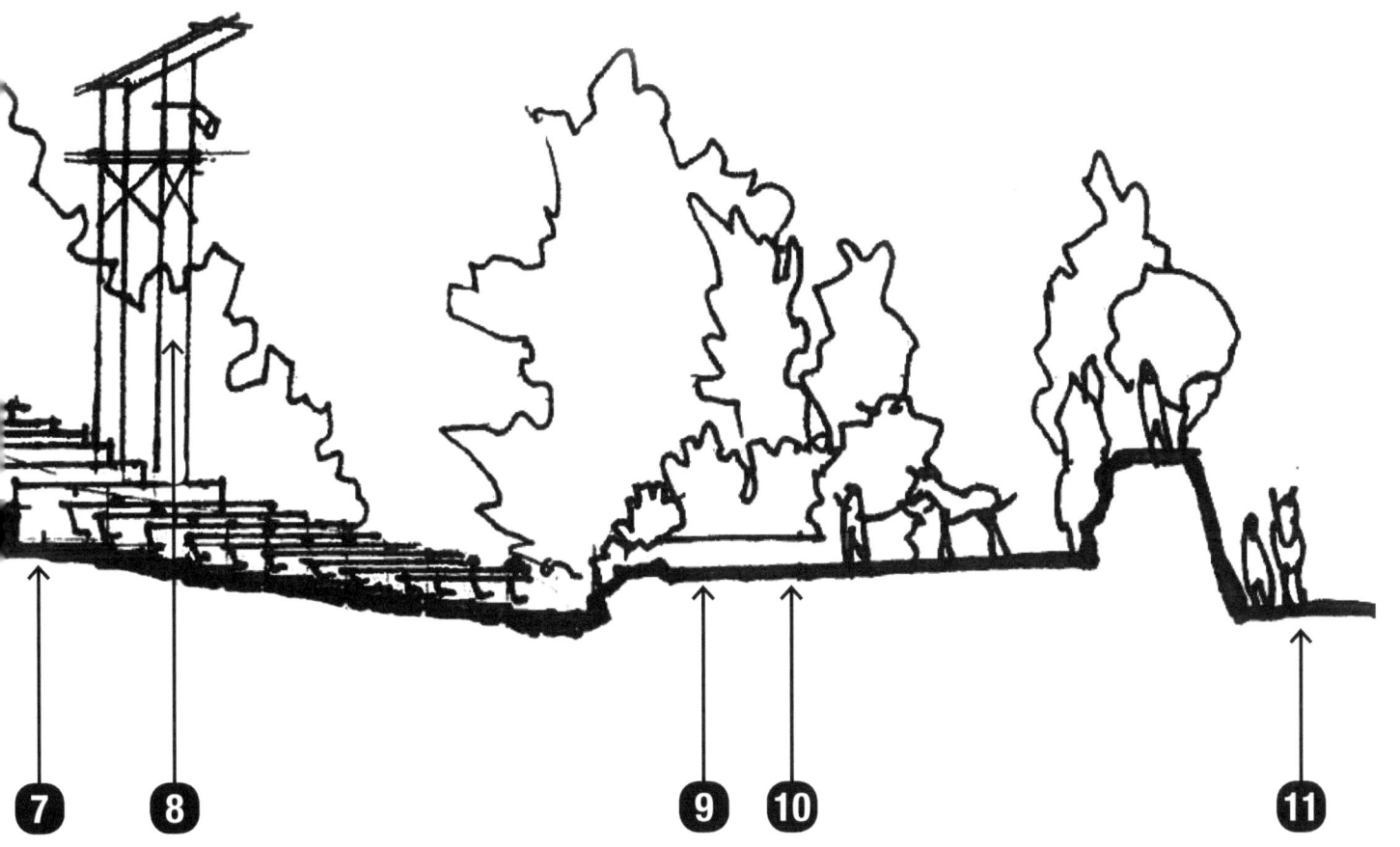

When an amphitheatre is used for a changing repertory of productions or presentations, the physical production elements are usually lighter and more stylized because they are constantly being changed. Each production or presentation is a separate artistic unit, often with different directors and designers, and they are rarely repeated in subsequent seasons. The types of productions that appear in such theatres range from Shakespeare festivals to Broadway musicals and plays or dance concerts. Some amphitheatres focus entirely on touring events such as the Minack Theatre in Cornwall, United Kingdom, or the Red Rocks Amphitheatre in Colorado. More often, amphitheatres that present changing attractions have adapted their facilities by adding some type of stage or audience covering to reduce the frequency of weather-related cancellations.

The two main advantages of the fully open amphitheatre are:

1. Both the capital and operating costs are lower than for other constructed outdoor theatres.
2. The special ambience of attending a performance under an open sky, at least in good weather, has a unique appeal for audiences.

The disadvantages are:

1. Regardless of the type of programming, the risk of weather-related cancellations and lost revenue is higher than with theatres that provide some level of weather protection. In some climates, such as Southern California, the risk of cancellations for inclement weather is negligible. In other climates, such as Mississippi, an open amphitheatre could risk losing 10 to 20% of their possible shows. Even when performances are not actually cancelled, threatening weather can seriously depress ticket sales.
2. Open amphitheatres cannot achieve the same quality of stage lighting and sound control as other types of outdoor theatres, primarily because of the limited positions for hanging lights and speakers. This can become a significant deterrent to attendance as audience expectations increase.
3. While maintenance costs are less for open amphitheatres, they are not negligible, and it is important that a theatre and its audience services not appear to be neglected or out of date. Audiences accustomed to 'home theatres' and air-conditioning have become less tolerant than those of past generations.
4. Theatres that produce the same production each season spend more on scenery and costumes initially because they have to last for a number of years. They also incur greater maintenance costs for these elements or risk their deterioration, which diminishes the effectiveness of the show.
5. Similarly, productions that play for decades risk becoming outdated if substantial, and sometimes expensive, efforts are not made to rejuvenate the show for contemporary audiences. This would be true regardless of the type of theatre facility housing the production, but the fact is that a significant percentage of open amphitheatres feature the historical or religious plays that are repeated annually.

In the opinion of the Institute of Outdoor Theatre, the disadvantages of the open amphitheatre model have come to outweigh its advantages. The combination of changing audience tastes and the theatre's complete vulnerability to weather and environmental events indicates to us that either the roofed stage or fully roofed models of outdoor theatre are more economical, flexible and capable of delivering a successful and sustainable performer-audience experience. In our view, open amphitheatres will continue to be useful for periodic outdoor performances but will experience increasingly difficult challenges as full-time seasonal theatres. Except for theatres located on spectacular natural sites or that represent an archaeological treasure, open air amphitheatre operators would be well advised to examine the feasibility of converting these theatres to one of the partial or fully roofed models discussed in this study.

Fig 38, 39, 40 / *Unto These Hills* is an outdoor historical drama at the 2,800-seat Mountainside Theatre in Cherokee, NC. It is the third oldest outdoor historical drama in the United States. The first version of the play was written by Kermit Hunter and opened on July 1, 1950.

Fig 41 / The Idaho Shakespeare Festival is a regional repertory theatre located in Boise, ID. The 770-seat Idaho Shakespeare Festival Amphitheater and Habitat Reserve is along the Boise River, on park lands. The theatre design by architects Brian Robinson, Eugene Angel and Joseph Michal LeMosh sited the theatre to take advantage of the topography and 'borrowed' landscape for a backdrop.

Fig 42 - 45/ The historical drama *Tecumseh!* takes advantage of the unique opportunities for outdoor theatre, including the use of real water bodies, fire, cannons, and horses to create a realistic experience. The stage and grounds were designed to match the play written by Allan W. Eckert, and the show has been running each summer at the 1,800-seat Sugarloaf Mountain Amphitheatre in Chillicothe, OH since 1973.

72

Fig 46-49 / Perhaps the most famous outdoor theatre venue in the United States is free to attend: the Public Theater's Shakespeare in the Park at the 1,800-seat Delacorte Theater is packed through the season, with patrons lining up six or eight hours early for tickets regardless of weather. Due to the vision of Joseph Papp, over five million people have attended the Shakespeare and other classical works since the theatre opened in 1962. Shakespeare in the Park, Central Park, New York City.

Fig 50-52 / Tuacahn Center for the Arts is located in the mouth of the Padre Canyon, in Ivins, UT. The 1,920-seat amphitheatre, designed by Leslie A. Stoker, was completed in 1995, and oriented to take advantage of the 1,500-foot cliffs as a backdrop. Tuacahn hosts a variety of Broadway shows in the summer season.

Fig 53/ Regent's Park Open Air Theatre, London, UK. Regent's Park Open Air Theatre, formally opened in 1933, is the oldest permanent outdoor theatre in Britain, with an annual 16-week season. The design of the theatre preserves sightlines through raked graded seats. Today the original deck chairs have been replaced with permanent seating.

Model #2: Roofed Stage with Open Amphitheatre

In this model the audience seating area is open to the sky with a built pavilion at the rear of the amphitheatre for the entry and front-of-house functions, and the performance area is a built structure including a stage with a roof that may extend into the backstage areas for dressing rooms, production shops, etc.

There are a number of advantages to be gained by roofing the stage:

- Performers in rehearsals and performances have some degree of protection from sun and rain. This is particularly beneficial to musicians and their instruments and the costumes and makeup of the performers.
- The structure allows lighting instruments and speakers to be located above the stage, which is far more effective than any position available for an open-air stage. There is no need for side lighting towers in this model, though many lighting designers will ask for them.
- As opposed to an earthen stage, the stage in this model is always a built structure supporting the roof. This makes it safer for dancers and much easier to use for scenic changes.
- The back wall and ceiling of the stage-roof structure act as an acoustical shell to focus and conserve the energy of sound and speech.
- Since the built stage can be very similar in its layout to the stage of an indoor theatre, its flexibility facilitates rapid changeovers and the efficient programming of different kinds of shows.
- All of these advantages make this model particularly useful for organizations that wish to produce multiple shows or to combine producing and presenting to maximize their programming. In the area of presenting, most musical acts—which comprise the majority of the touring market—will not perform under an open sky because of the threat to their instruments and exposed electronic equipment.
- These elements provide the audience with a much better quality of performance experience while retaining that 'under the stars' ambience during good weather.
- Finally, because the stage house is basically a three-sided box, it can be used as a secure, weatherproof storage area for equipment by closing up the front of the stage at the end of the season.

The chief disadvantage of this model is that it is more expensive to construct (capital expense) and maintain (operating expense) than an open amphitheatre with an open stage. If the audience seating area is located on a natural slope that provides good sightlines to the stage, the additional construction cost will be primarily limited to the stage house. If elevating the audience area to a proper slope in addition to the construction of the stage building, the cost will be higher. While all theatres need to be maintained, built structures are more expensive to repair than natural landscapes. In planning a new theatre, both the capital and operating costs must be weighed against the potential for additional revenues from enhanced programming and the extension of the performance season that a roofed stage provides.

Fig 54 / Roofed Stage with Open Amphitheatre Plan Legend:

1. Pavilion
2. Box Office
3. Concessions
4. Office
5. Storage
6. Men
7. Women
8. Electrical
9. Control Booth
10. Light/Sound Locks
11. Amphitheatre—1,000 Seats
12. Cross Aisle—ADA Access
13. Main Stage
14. Side Stage
15. Off Stage
16. Crossover

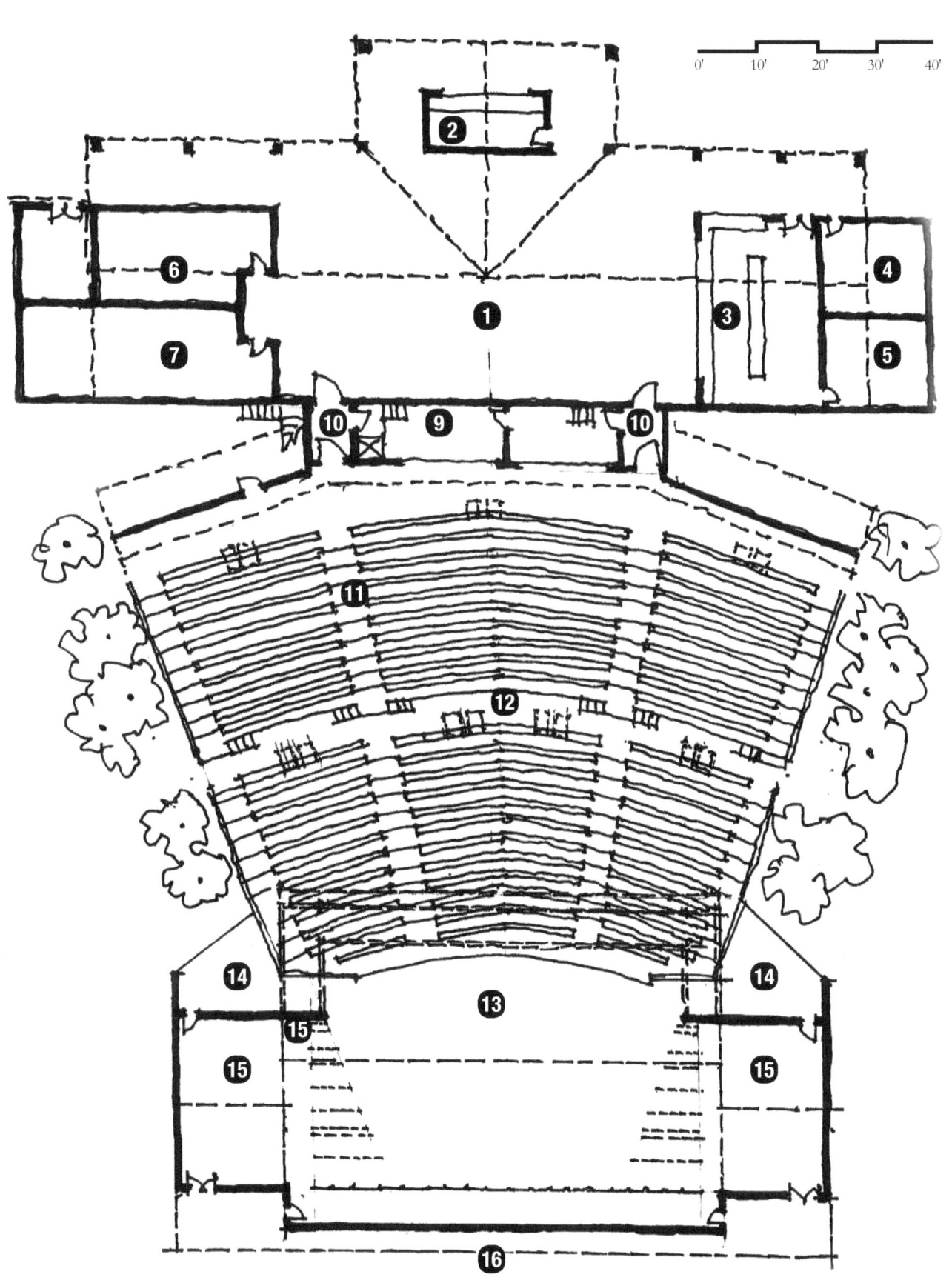

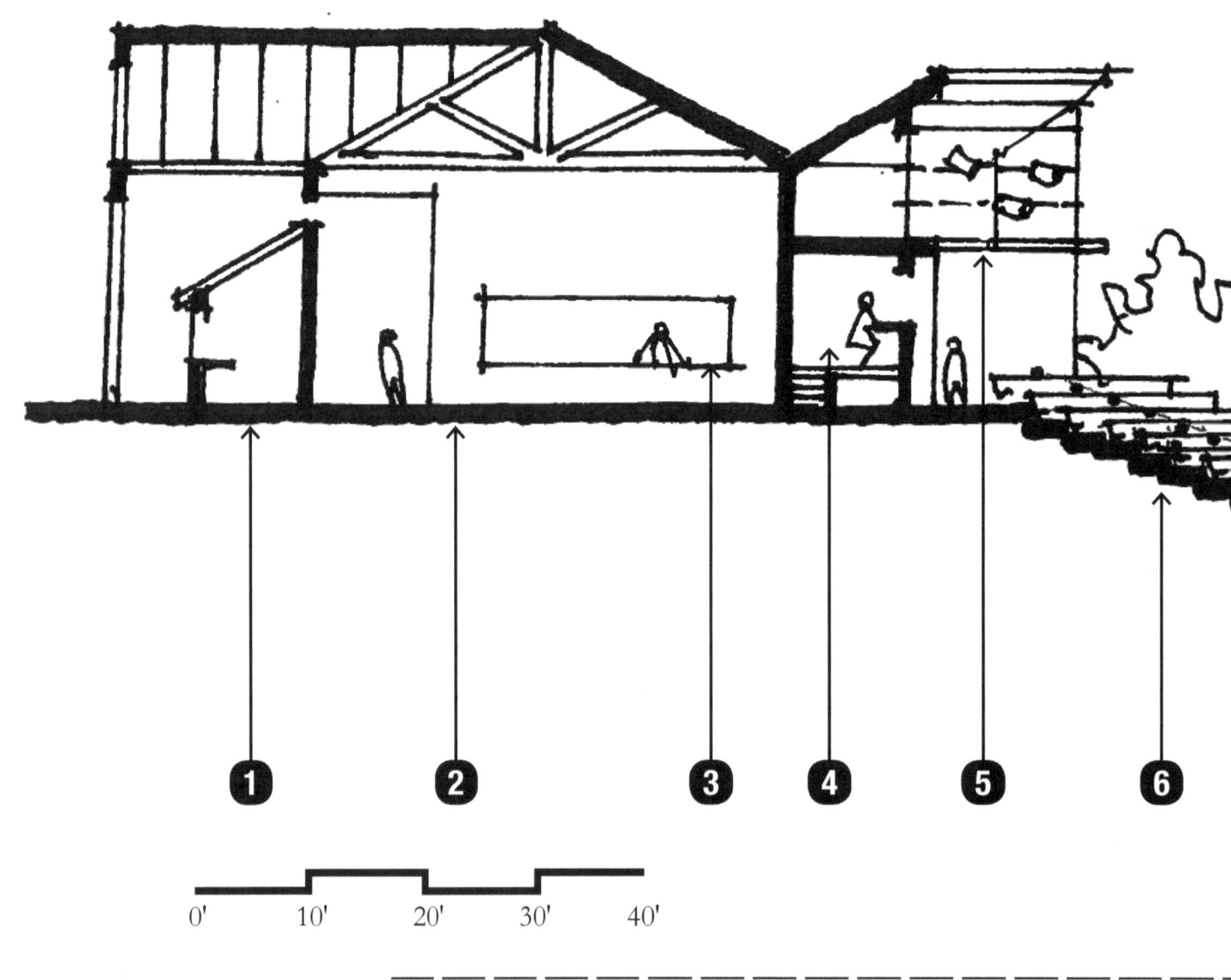

0' 10' 20' 30' 40'

Fig 55 / Roofed Stage with Open Amphitheatre Section Legend:

1. Box Office
2. Pavilion
3. Concessions
4. Control Booth
5. Lighting Deck
6. Amphitheatre—1,000 Seats
7. Cross Aisle—ADA Access
8. Apron
9. Proscenium—60'x30' Opening
10. Main Stage
11. Crossover

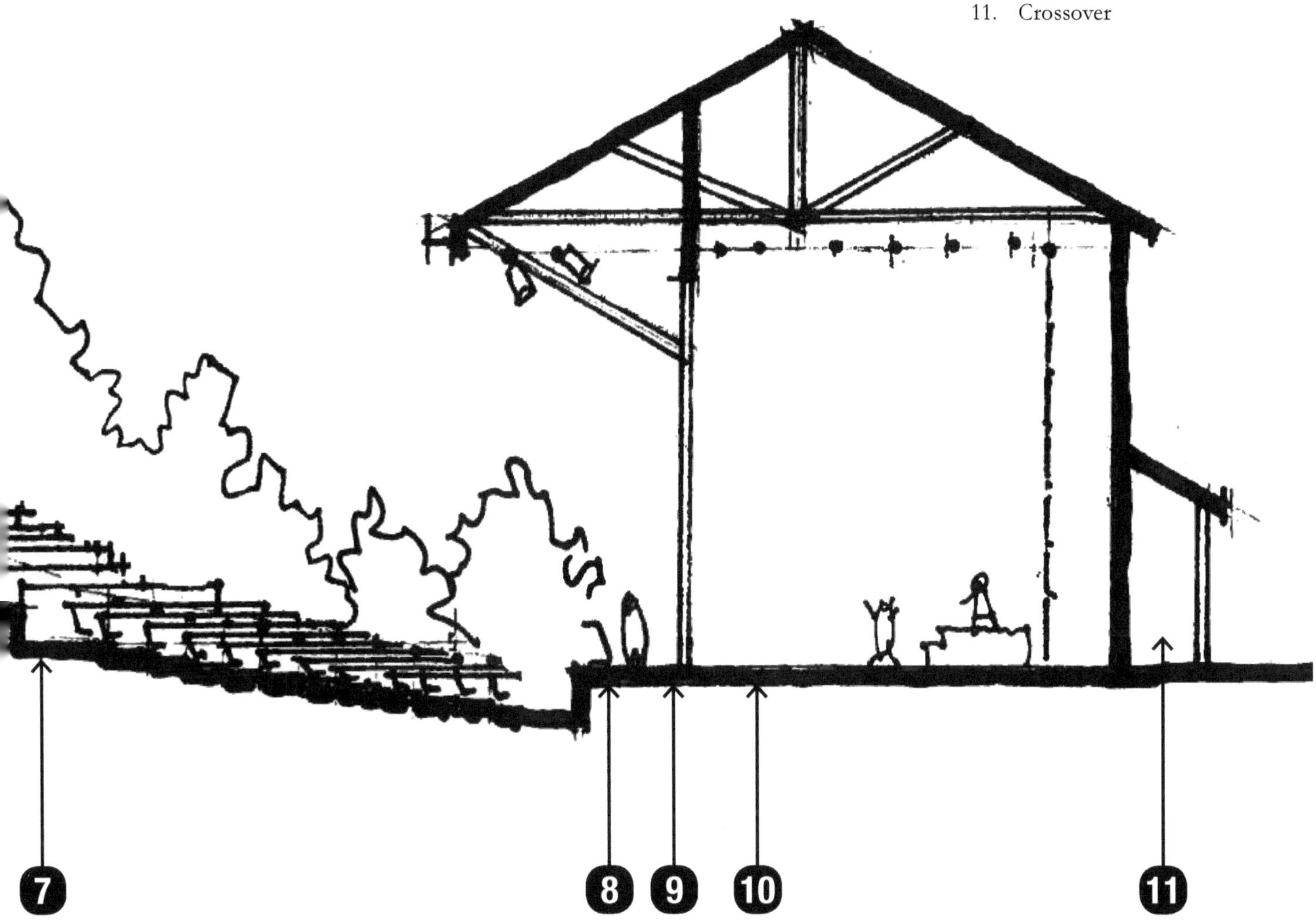

Fig 56-58 / The Smith-Ritch Point Theatre is a 722-seat open amphitheatre with a roofed stage along the Guadalupe River in Ingram, TX. In addition to the outdoor facility, the Hill Country Arts Foundation also has a small 150-seat indoor space for the winter season. This facility was designed by architect Barry Moore, coauthor of this book, in 1983.

1936

2007

Fig 59-61 / The Waldbühne (literally translated as woodland stage) amphitheatre was originally built for the 1936 Summer Olympics in Berlin, designed by Werner March. With a rather tumultuous history in the '50s and '60s, the venue was renewed with a concert by Bob Marley in 1980 establishing it as a rock venue. The architectural fabric canopy was added in 1982. Architectural canopies are an excellent way to retrofit existing amphitheatres.

Model #3: Roofed Stage and Amphitheatre

There are two historical precedents for these types of theatres, which add a partial or full roof cover over the audience area as well as maintaining a roofed stage. In some of the ancient Roman theatres, a retractable fabric roof called a *vela* could be deployed over the audience to protect it from the rain or sun. In Shakespeare's England, where audiences and actors had to contend with London's unpredictable and rainy climate, the Globe Theatre and its counterparts were designed with a roof over the stage and had covered seating for about 2,000 people, with another 1,000 standing in the yard under the open sky.

In these theatres today, the audience roof should connect seamlessly to the stage covering. It can then either extend over part of the audience or all the way back to the pavilion at the front-of-house, forming one continuous structure. The edges of the roof are supported by structural posts.

There are many more advantageous locations for hanging lighting and sound equipment in this model than there are in the roofed stage model. The combined stage and roof structure helps to contain and focus the sound of the event, making it superior to the other models for both unamplified and amplified sound. More sophisticated audio systems capable of producing directional sound effects also function well in this model. Some theatres of this type that present musicals or music concerts add lawn seating areas at the sides or rear of the theatre with additional speakers broadcasting to those locations. Audience members can then enjoy blanket seating and picnics at a lower cost and still be able to hear and see the show. If the theatre has a partial roof, such as the one pictured at the Iroquois Amphitheatre in Louisville, KY, where approximately half of the seats are covered, audience members can choose whether to sit under shelter or the open sky. Where blowing rain is a significant problem, some theatres have installed vinyl strip curtain walls around the perimeter of the audience roof, which can be opened or closed on traveler tracks as needed. Upholstered seating with weather-resistant fabric is also possible. For certain theatres that cannot program during the day because of heat and strong sunshine, the shade of a roofed auditorium may enable the presentation of daytime events. Recent research on insect control has also found that breezes as slow as five miles per hour create a headwind sufficiently strong to prevent mosquitos from entering an area. Although we are not aware of any outdoor theatres yet using this information, it is theoretically possible that large ceiling fans installed under an audience roof might be sufficient to render the area mosquito free.

Because there is a good deal more structure in this model, its construction costs will be considerably higher than only roofing the stage area. Depending on local building, safety and fire codes it may be necessary to add house lights above the audience, and the structure may need to have fire sprinklers. If destructive pests, such as squirrels and nesting birds, are prevalent, it may be necessary to design to prevent nest building and roosting. Access for technicians to the lighting and sound positions may require catwalks, and maintenance workers will also need to be able to reach critical areas. Maintenance will also be more expensive since all structures deteriorate over time and need to be repaired.

Fig 62 / Roofed Stage and Partially Roofed Amphitheatre Plan Legend:

1. Pavilion
2. Box Office
3. Concessions
4. Office
5. Storage
6. Men
7. Women
8. Electrical
9. Control Booth
10. Light/Sound Lock
11. Amphitheatre—1,000 Seats
12. Roofed Parterre
13. Cross Aisle—ADA Access
14. Lighting Catwalk Above
15. Roof Support/Access
16. Line of Roof Above
17. Main Stage
18. Side Stage
19. Off Stage
20. Crossover

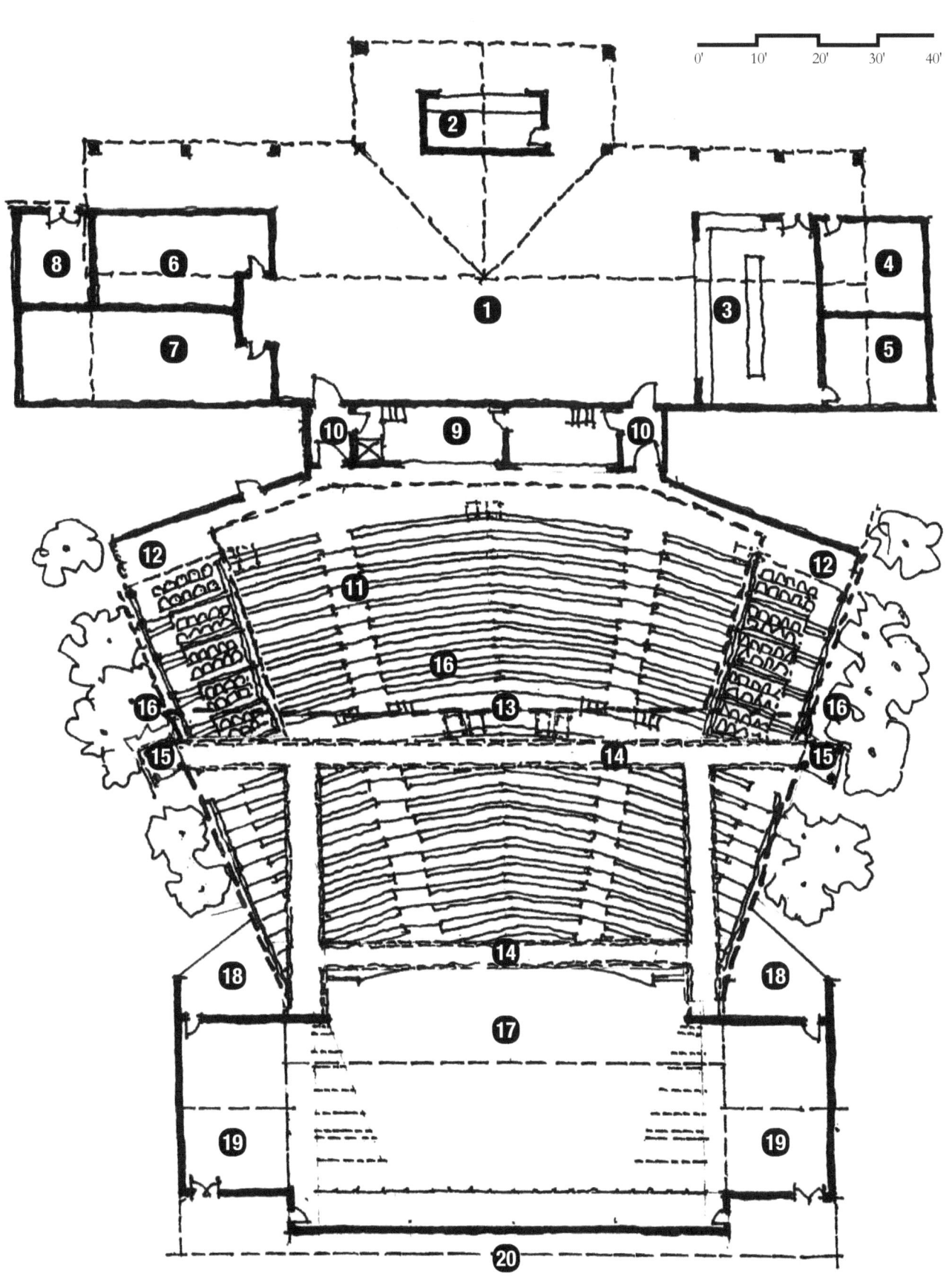

Fig 63 / Roofed Stage and Partially
Roofed Amphitheatre Section Legend:

1. Box Office
2. Pavilion
3. Concessions
4. Control Booth
5. Amphitheatre—1,000 Seats
6. Line of Roof Over Parterre
7. Cross Aisle—ADA Access
8. Roof Support/Access
9. Lighting Catwalk
10. Apron
11. Proscenium—60'x30' Opening
12. Main Stage
13. Crossover

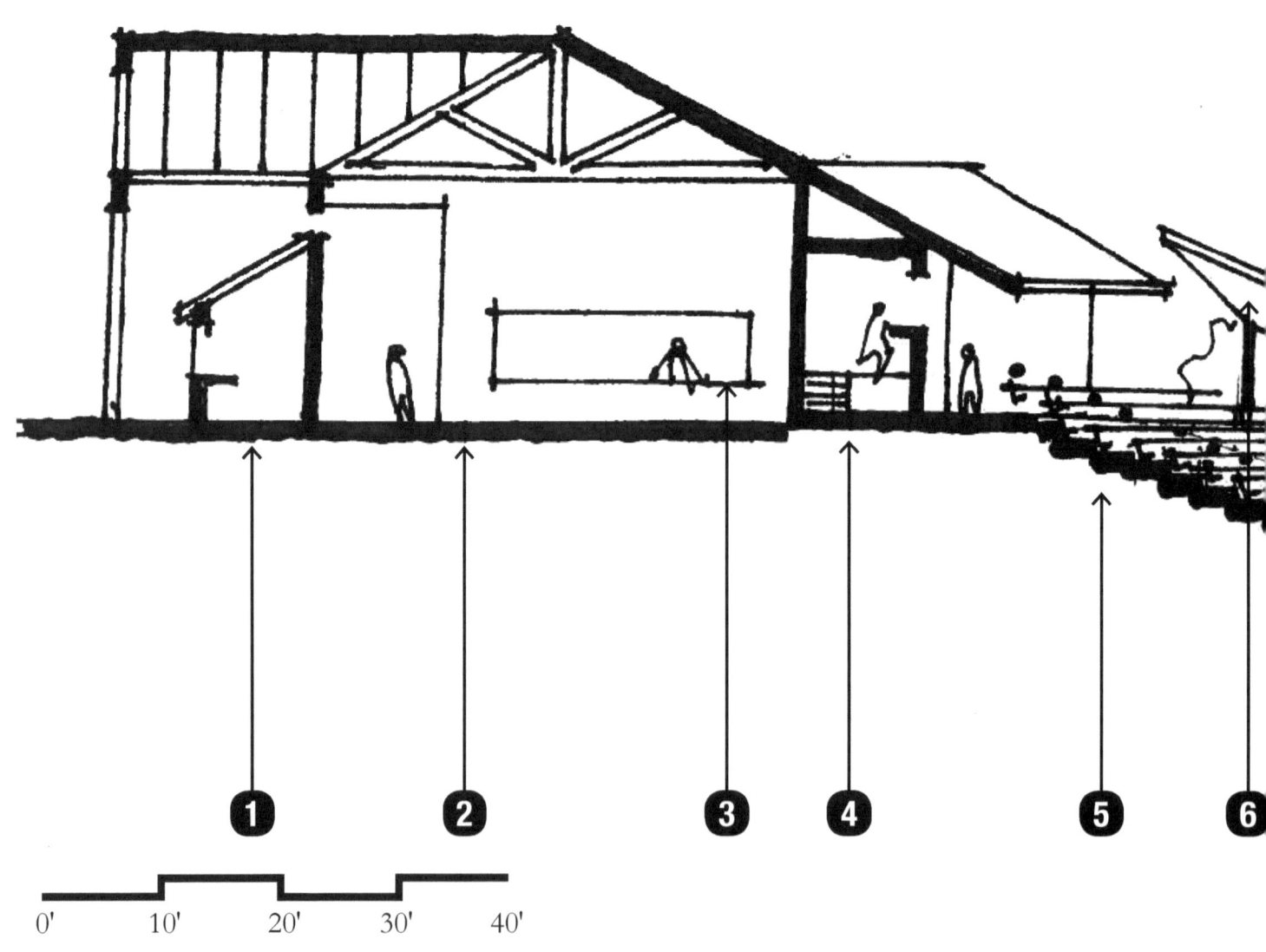

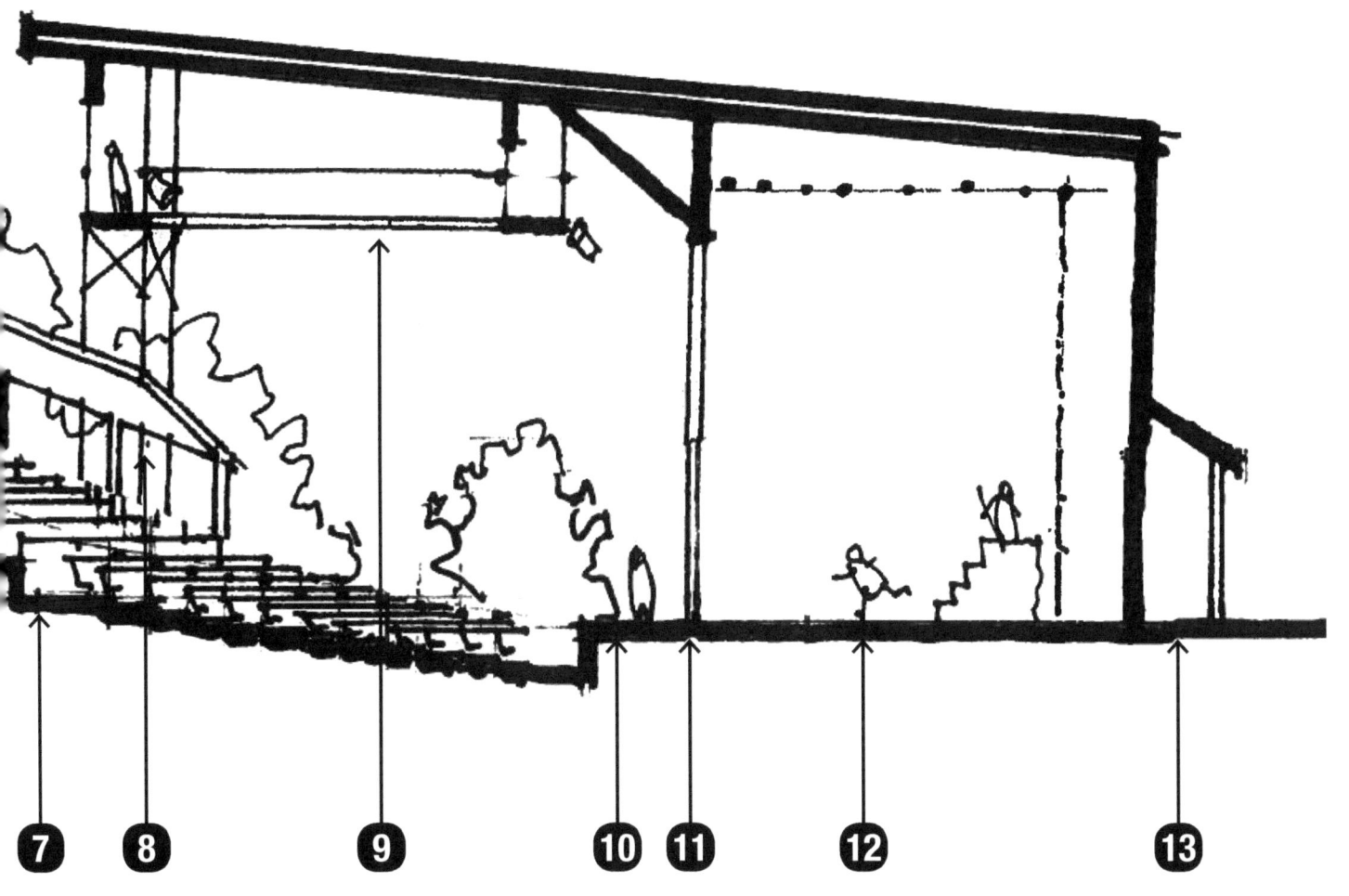

Tenting

Theatres wishing to shelter their audiences are increasingly turning to architectural fabrics as an attractive and sometimes less expensive alternative to hard structure. We have included several illustrations using this approach to indicate the range of designs that are currently available with this material. There are both permanent architectural fabric systems intended to be up year round, and seasonal structures, which must be taken down and stored in the winter. When evaluating the costs of the temporary approach, theatres should be careful to include the installation and off-season storage costs as well as the initial purchase price. One especially large installation in Canada that uses two tents costs approximately $600,000 to set up, disassemble and store their facility each year. That expense should be compared to the annual maintenance for a 'permanent' structure, which, on average, costs as much over twenty years as the cost of the original building.

Besides cost, the chief disadvantage of the roofed audience model is aesthetic; it loses some of the magic and romance of outdoor performance. It has been observed and documented that many people and families who go to outdoor theatre rarely attend other theatre events. Surveys show that the informality of the events and the ability to bring children (and sometimes pets) have a special appeal for these attenders. To the extent that a theatre looks and feels more like an indoor theatre without walls, some of that appeal may be lost. At the same time, we must note that virtually all of the very large outdoor venues combine covered and uncovered seating, and that they are extremely well attended.

For these reasons, we recommend that organizations considering building or renovating a theatre to include an audience roof utilize the partial roof solution and offer both covered and uncovered seating options for the public. During inclement weather, when attendance will be somewhat reduced in any case, people will choose to sit under the shelter and the show can proceed. In good weather, the audience will sit according to their individual preferences. The full or partially roofed amphitheatre and stage can produce or present virtually any program that can be done in an indoor theatre. This makes it the most flexible model we have evaluated and the one with the fewest limitations. It is also the most expensive to build and maintain. Whether that expense is justified will depend a great deal on the market of potential ticket buyers and the types of programs they can be motivated to attend.

Fig 64 / Roofed Stage and Roofed Amphitheatre Plan Legend:

1. Pavilion
2. Box Office
3. Concessions
4. Office
5. Storage
6. Men
7. Women
8. Electrical
9. Control Booth
10. Light/Sound Lock
11. Amphitheatre—1000 Seats
12. Cross Aisle—ADA Access
13. Lighting Catwalk Above
14. Roof Support/Access
15. Line of Roof Above
16. Main Stage
17. Side Stage
18. Off Stage
19. Crossover

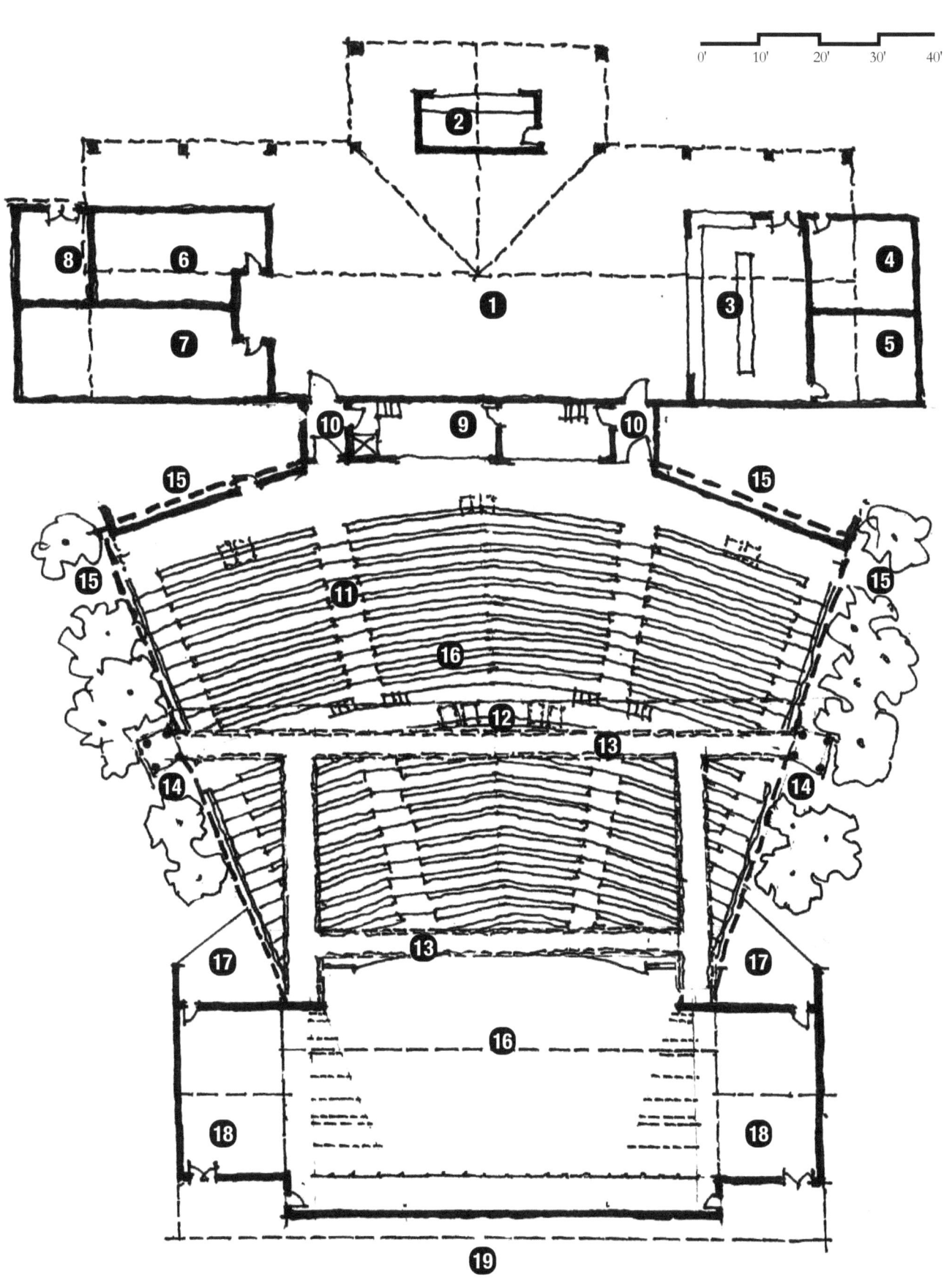

Fig 65 / Roofed Stage and Roofed Amphitheatre Section Legend:

1. Box Office
2. Pavilion
3. Concessions
4. Control Booth
5. Amphitheatre—1,000 Seats
6. Cross Aisle—ADA Access
7. Roof Support/Access
8. Lighting Catwalk
9. Apron
10. Proscenium—60'x30' Opening
11. Main Stage
12. Crossover

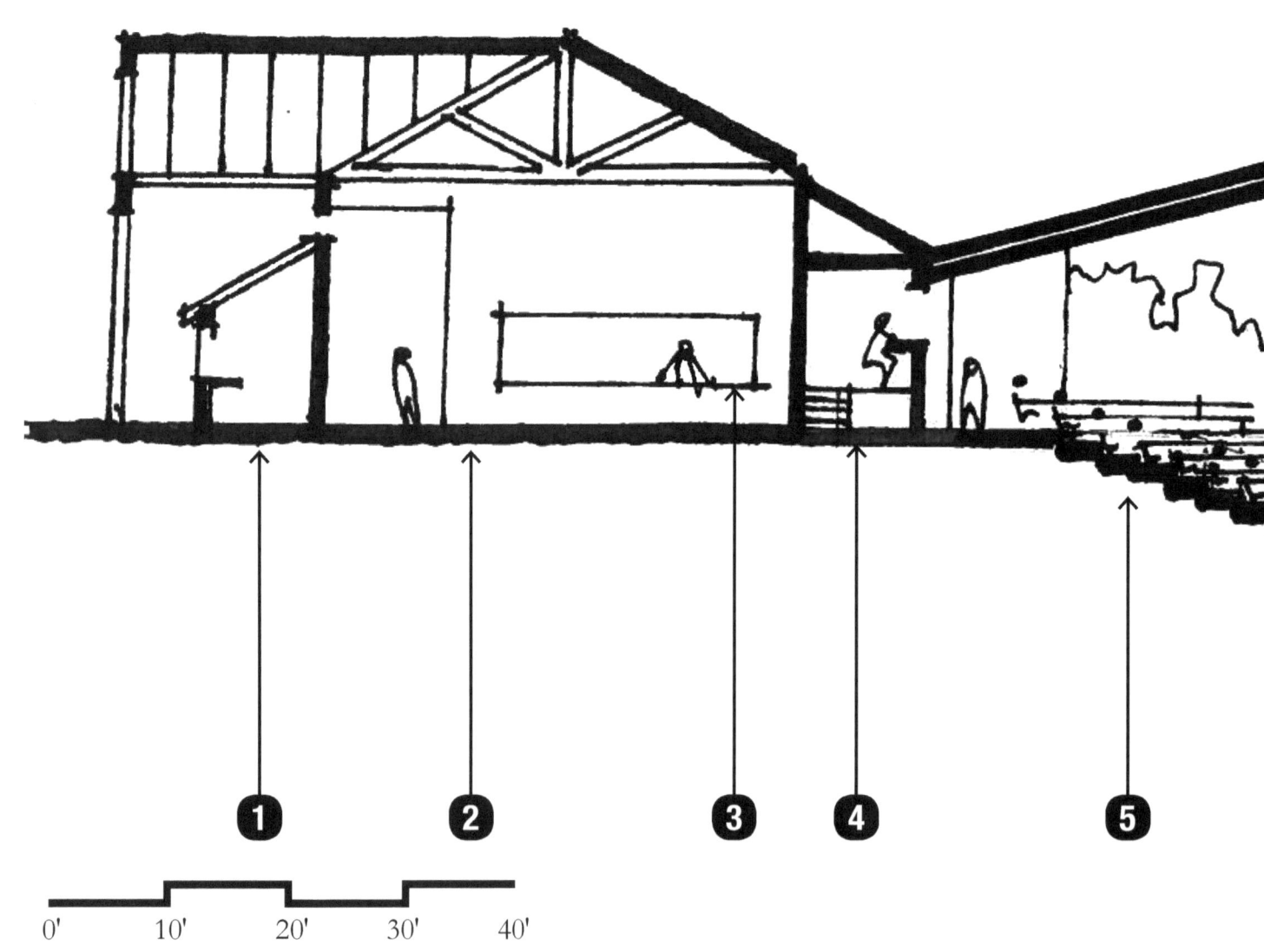

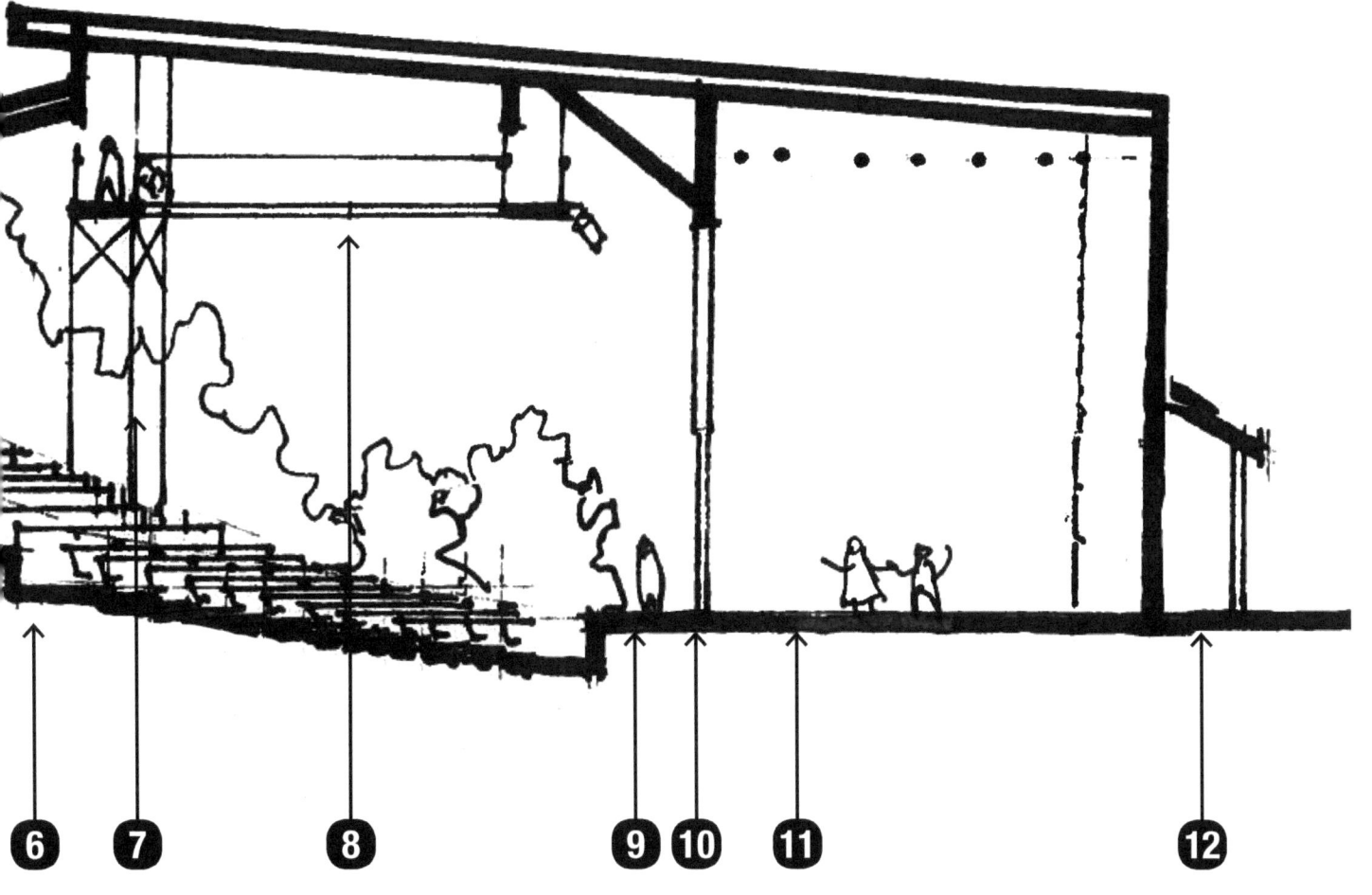

Fig 66-68 / Shakespeare's legendary Globe Theatre was probably the first outdoor theatre to solve the issue of weather by putting the majority of the audience and performers under roof shelters while leaving an opening in the center of the structure to admit daylight for illumination. A modern reconstruction of the theatre, named 'Shakespeare's Globe' and located 750 feet from the original in London, opened in 1997 after a long iterative design process. The roofed stage and balconies surround the standing-room-only pit. More recently, with the Bengt Sjostrom and New Swan Theatres (Figs. 84 and 88), this form is being reinterpreted in new and exciting ways.

Fig 69 / The Miller Outdoor Theatre in Houston, TX, can seat 1,705 under the shed, with space on a sloped lawn with a capacity for an additional 4,500 patrons. Over the years successive outdoor theatre facilities have existed on the site, with the current roof configuration designed by Eugene Werlin in 1968. Free music and theatrical performances are held for the Houston public for the eight-month season, attracting almost a half million attendees a year.

Fig 70, 71 / The Ravinia Pavilion in Highland Park, IL, is the oldest continuously running outdoor music venue in the United States, hosting the Chicago Symphony Orchestra since 1936. In addition to the Pavilion that seats 3,350, the grounds of the rest of Ravinia Park are also used by theatre and concert goers, who are allowed to set up full picnics including alcoholic beverages. The grounds can absorb additional capacities up to 15,000 attendees. The current pavilion was designed by John Augur Holabird.

Fig 72 / The Iroquois Amphitheater, in Louisville, KY. Located in the heart of the Fredrick Law Olmsted–designed Iroquois Park, the original 1938 Works Progress Administration (WPA) amphitheatre was open to the sky. With the redesign and restoration, opened in 2003, Bravura Architecture balanced historic preservation with modernizing the facility. The result is a more resilient and programmable space.

Model #4: Temporary Theatres

Impromptu temporary theatres probably pre-date any permanent theatre structure, but we see the first visual representations of them during the medieval and renaissance periods. The mystery and miracle plays of the middle ages appeared on pageant wagons as early as the tenth century, and the traveling Italian troupes of commedia dell'arte performed in marketplaces throughout Europe during the 16th and 17th Centuries.

A common type of outdoor theatre is the portable, temporary or seasonal performance environment that may be used for anything from a few days to a few months before moving to different locations or going into storage for the off-season. These theatres vary a great deal and can range from an open park lawn with little or no structure to fully developed seating and staging areas under custom-designed tents.

At the end of the performance period, temporary theatres are dismantled and stored for the off-season. They are typically set up on property that is not owned by the producing organization, so all the arrangements must be made for power, technical support, dressing rooms, audience amenities and front-of-house.

Because of this nomadic model, most organizations performing in temporary theatres place a high value on portability, ease of setup and compactness of storage volume. Motorized stages or 'showmobiles' and tents are often used to accomplish these objectives. Built structures tend to consist of platforms, scaffolding and trusses that can be easily disassembled and transported.

Achieving a high quality of technical support, convenient facilities for the performers and comfortable audience amenities is hard to accomplish in temporary theatres but not impossible. More elaborate installations such as Cirque du Soleil or Vancouver's Bard on the Beach show that this can be done but not without very significant expense. Cirque du Soleil produces spectacles worldwide and frequently performs in its 'Village on Wheels.' Bard on the Beach operates seasonally under an elaborate set of tents that are stored during the winter.

Fig 73 / Pageant wagon for the Coventry cycle, c. 1400.

Fig 74 / Karel Dujardins, commedia dell'arte show, dated 1657.

More often, the charm of the seasonal theatre is in its informal quality: sitting on blankets and folding chairs with picnics, children and dogs during the afternoon or in the evening under the stars. Whether they are elaborately or simply produced, these types of theatres embody, perhaps better than any of the others, the kind of family-oriented, close to home, frequently impromptu cultural experiences that help define summer in small towns and large cities alike.

Because of their portable nature, many of these theatres have no ticketed admission and rely on audience donations coupled with grants and sponsorships for their revenue. They may or may not have concession operations. Often they are invited to appear by local arts councils or parks departments. In some cases, an established indoor theatre will produce outdoor performances in a temporary theatre as an additional way of serving its community and building support.

Fig 75 / The Hudson Valley Shakespeare Festival at Boscobel, in upstate New York, uses temporary architectural fabric canopies.

Fig 76 / The San Francisco Shakespeare Festival is able to reach out to many communities by being portable, setting up in different parks and public spaces around the Bay Area.

Fig 77 / Bard on the Beach Shakespeare Festival is hosted at Vanier Park in Vancouver, Canada. Set up in a circus-style format, the flexibility of the design allows for constant adaptation and reinterpretation.

Fig 78 / Some of the most provoking productions can be place and time specific interventions, such as the work by Lucia Neare's Theatrical Wonders in Seattle, WA.

Model #5: Hybrid Theatres

Fig 79-82 / Rotating Amphitheatres: left: Pyynikki Summer Theatre (Finland, 1959); right: Český Krumlov (Czech Republic, 1958).

A hybrid theatre is one that has transplanted elements from one or more of the theatre models already discussed into an existing theatre or developed into a new kind of theatre.

Some examples of transplants for existing theatres could be:

- Adding a truss span to an open amphitheatre stage to hang lights and speakers
- Using architectural fabric to provide a temporary pavilion, concessions or dining area for a permanent theatre
- Renovating an open amphitheatre by covering the stage or a portion of the audience seating area, either with a hard structure or tenting

There are a number of possible combinations like these, which could be used to adapt or improve a pre-existing theatre.

Builders and architects have also experimented with uniquely different types of theatres. We should expect to see more of these as new building materials are developed and computer-assisted design continues to expand the range of what is possible. Here are three examples of particularly innovative facilities.

The original theatres of this type were developed over fifty years ago. There is a similar theatre in Quebec. The audience seating area is built on a turntable and rotates to different 'stages' around a perimeter of up to 270 degrees, each of which can have a different setting or scene. Performers can also travel from one stage to the next while the audience rotates to keep them in view. Audience seating is accessed either from the front or from stairways at the rear of the structure. The audience area can be open to the elements or have its own roof with built-in lighting and audio speakers, and the performance stages on the perimeter are unroofed. The existing examples of the rotating amphitheatres are designed for play production, opera and dance, and the effect is quite dramatic. The theatre at Český Krumlov performs an average of 80 plays per season and is an extremely popular tourist attraction as well as an excellent theatre venue.

Plan   Section

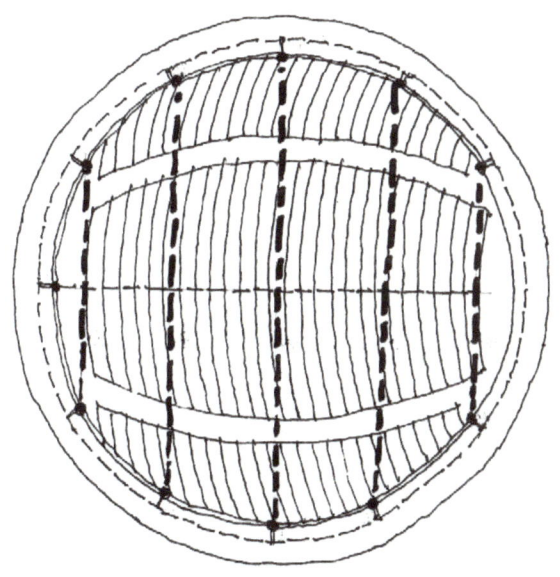
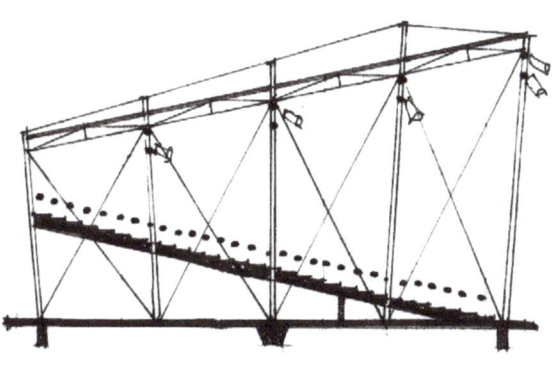

Fig 83 / **Recycled Materials:** The New Swan Theater at UC Irvine, CA. Although the interior of this theatre looks conventional, the exterior is constructed of recycled materials, and the set-up time is surprisingly short. The website includes a video showing the two-day load-in from start to finish. Much of the interior is assembled from scaffolding and trusses, keeping the amount of space needed for storage to a minimum. This theatre was designed by Luke Hegel-Cantarella, assistant professor of scenic design at the UC Irvine drama department, and constructed by the department's technical director. It was subject to rigorous city and university inspections and can withstand 85-mph winds and an 8.0 earthquake. Seating only 125 audience members, this structure would not be large enough for many theatres, but it illustrates how the availability of new building materials and imagination can combine to create new, unexpected places for theatre performance.

Fig 84, 85 / Inflatable Amphitheatres: The first example of this type is the newly designed Ark Nova inflatable concert hall, which was developed in partnership with the Lucerne Festival to tour the flood-ravaged areas of Japan in 2013. It was designed by Indian-born United Kingdom–based artist Anish Kapoor and Japanese architect Arata Isozaki. Although intended as a concert hall, the structure could easily be adapted for theatre performances.

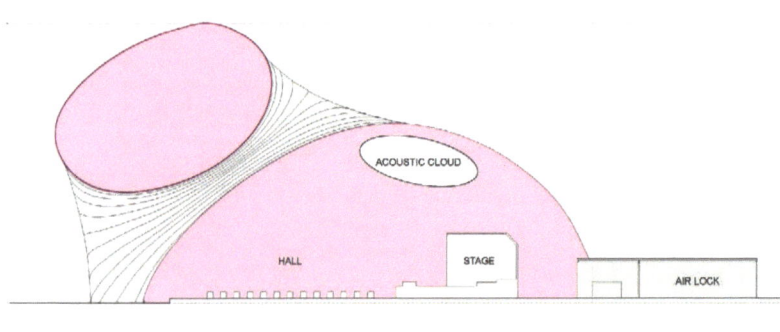

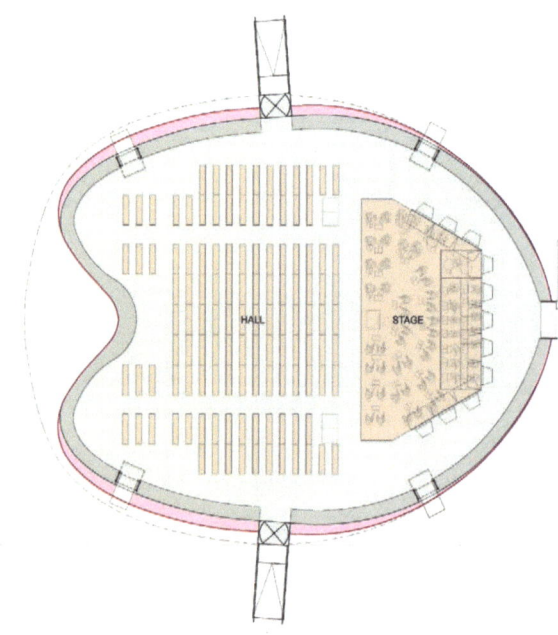

Fig 86-89 / Retractable Roof: Although sports facilities have been designed with retractable roofs for many years, this solution has not been used by theatres very often. This is because of the high costs of such systems and the fact that theatre revenues are quite small in comparison with the ticket and television revenues of professional sports. We have, however, identified at least two recent examples: the Bengt Sjostrom Starlight Theatre designed by Studio Gang Architects is located in Rockford, IL, and pictured here. Also, currently in design, the new Shakespeare Theatre at the Utah Shakespeare Theatre in Cedar City, UT, is planned with a retractable roof. Whether new design techniques and materials will make such systems more affordable in the future remains to be seen, but they would certainly have wide appeal if that were the case. In the case of the Bengt Sjostrom Starlight Theatre, the side walls remain open even when the roof is closed.

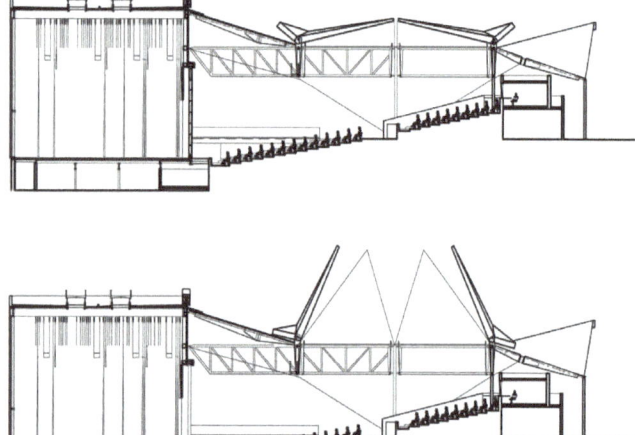

Fig 90-93 / Open wall: Designed by architect William Rawn, theatre consultant Auerbach Pollock Friedlander, acoustician Lawrence Kirkegaard and the landscape architecture firm SWA Group, Weill Hall at Sonoma State in Rohnert Park, CA, was designed to replicate the intimacy and acoustics of Vienna's Musikverein while also being able to open up to a large audience on a terraced lawn beyond the hall.

Site-Specific Productions

The term 'site-specific' can have several meanings related to theatre productions. A common meaning refers to a theatre that has been built in a specific location because of the relationship between the performance and the place. Theatre productions that commemorate specific historic events and are constructed on or near the actual historical site are often referred to as site-specific. The restored Globe Theatre in London, England, is site-specific in a slightly different sense: it is sited in the part of London where the original Globe was located in the 16th century. Yet another type of site-specific theatre occurs where there is no physical theatre facility at all.

Throughout the world of theatre performance, there is an increasing trend of staging what is often a one-time-only event in a non-theatre location that has been chosen for that purpose. This location may be selected for its appropriateness to the play (such as staging *A Midsummer Night's Dream* in a garden or forest setting), or because of some other ambience or factor that is part of the production concept. These events range from conventional plays and musicals to guerilla theatre, improvisations, and flash mobs. Forests, abandoned churches, lakes, city streets, vineyards, warehouses, malls, wharf sides, parking lots, beaches and parks are all places where this type of site-specific theatre occurs.

Obviously these sites have little or nothing in common with each other, but they still require some level of planning to be used effectively. Audiences have to arrive and depart, see and hear the theatre piece, and be able to relieve themselves. Actors often need to get into their costumes somewhere and enter and exit the place of performance. The theatre organization may want to sell tickets or concessions; the audience's safety and accessibility are important; and weather is still a factor. The site itself should be evaluated both from the artistic point of view and the basic characteristics of its landscape (hydrology, orientation, etc.), which could interfere with a good audience experience. The challenge of producing a successful site-specific event is to plan for these basic necessities without compromising the fresh, unconventional setting that helps create the uniqueness of the event. Even if part of the point of a site is to create a level of discomfort or awkwardness for the audience, the experience should be intentional rather than accidental. With this in mind, planners of site-specific events would do well to familiarize themselves with the basic requirements of all outdoor theatre facilities and consider how best to adapt those requirements to their event.

Fig 94/ The Walking Theatre Company, Argyll, Scotland, UK. This company integrates their shows with the sites and landscapes of Scotland, from playgrounds to forests, creating unique, low cost, and award-winning productions.

Fig 95-101 / **Vernacular theatre installation:** The 'Forest Pavilion,' designed by Eric Bunge and Mimi Hoang of nACHITECTS, was inspired by the traditional bamboo construction techniques of the local indigenous Amis tribe of Hualien, Taiwan. Tribal members completed the construction in 2011. This structure served the Masdi Art Festival for opening and closing ceremonies, as well as performance. This structure has a gentle touch, minimizing impact on the land as well as maximizing use of renewable resources, creating an interesting and dynamic performance space.

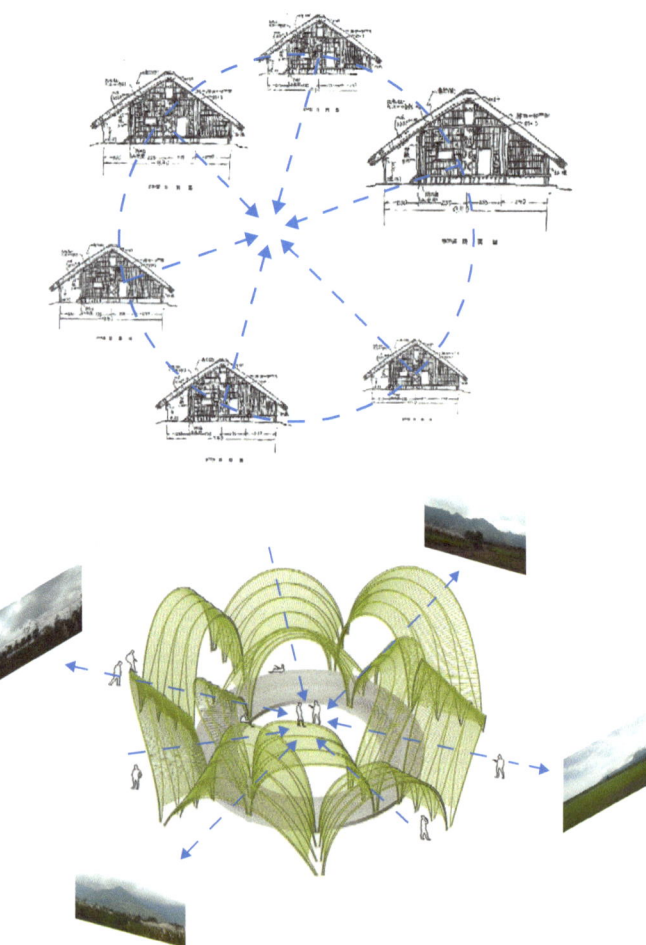

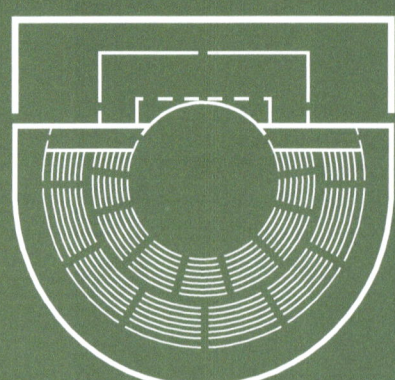

Chapter 6

Designing and Building a New Theatre

The Client and Design Team

Outdoor theatres have been designed and built by people with different types of expertise, including architects, landscape architects, contractors, set designers, and engineers. Because funding is often scarce and outdoor facilities seem to be simpler than indoor theatres, groups are often tempted to put as little money as possible into these facilities and find someone who can copy an existing theatre or follow a simple 'design-build' process. But even for experienced architects and contractors, designing and constructing an effective new outdoor theatre facility can be a surprisingly complex endeavor. Unless the theatre is going to be located in a metropolitan area, few if any local architects or builders will have designed or constructed one before. The facility will probably be the single largest capital investment that the organization will make, and it should be expected to last for several decades as well as be adaptable for changing needs and tastes in entertainment that will occur in the future.

Further complicating the process, many new theatre groups do not have an experienced theatre manager when they are beginning to plan their facility. If that lack of internal expertise is combined with a designer or contractor who has never built a theatre, the result may be seriously deficient in any number of ways and compromise the ability of the organization to fulfill its mission, even potentially exposing the organization to lawsuits. Once a theatre has been completed, it is very difficult and expensive to correct its mistakes.

For all these reasons, it makes sense for an organization to assemble as much expertise as possible in a facility design/construction team and carefully evaluate the credentials and experience of each team member. We use the word 'team' intentionally: there are a variety of kinds of expertise, and the best results will be obtained by gathering a group of specialists who can complement one another. This design team should work closely with the artistic and management leadership of the theatre organization. For organizations planning a facility for a specific play, such as a history or religious play, the management of the organization should also seek the input of the playwright, director and designer(s). The types of professionals that should be considered for the design/construction team are as follows:

Facility Design

Architects, Landscape Architects, Engineers: For any project involving a substantial 'built' structure, architects are typically the most experienced professionals available. Large architectural firms may have landscape architects within the firm for site design, or a landscape architect may be sub-contracted for that work. If the project consists largely of design to an outdoor site and the built structures are less important, a landscape architectural firm may be the lead firm. In this case, an architect can be subcontracted for the buildings. Whatever the hierarchy, the facility design for an outdoor theatre should have the separate expert input of an architect, a site designer and an engineering team.

Theatre Program

Theatre Consultants, Management Consultants: In building terms, the word 'program' has two different meanings.

One definition involves the detailed description of all the spaces of the facility, how they are supposed to function, what the relationships of the different parts should be, and what kinds of systems and equipment will be needed for its function. Typically, the theatre consultant develops this 'building program' in close consultation with the client. The theatre consultant is sometimes a member of the architect's design team and, in other cases, reports directly to the client. Whether this role is performed by a single consultant or a theatre consulting firm, their responsibility is to provide both the client and the architect with detailed lists of the functions and relationships of space and all theatrical equipment and systems. Theatre consultants are an integral part of the design team, evaluating early (concept) designs and closely involved with the project until its completion. It is important for the theatre consultants to spend considerable time with the theatre client so all parties understand exactly how the theatre is expected to function and what types of programs will be produced.

The second definition of 'program' involves the early projection of how the facility will operate, what types of performances will be presented, budget projections, and how many administrative and operations personnel will be required. If the theatre organization has an executive director or professional producer already on its staff, a separate management consultant may not be necessary. But if that is not the case, a management consultant who understands how theatres function is also important. Some of the worst oversights in theatre design occur because insufficient thought has been given to audience amenities, opportunities for earned income, office space, communications, computer equipment, ticketing facilities and a host of other features that will directly affect the financial success and efficiency of the theatre.

Design-Build

Contractors: An alternative process to the one described above is the design-build process. As the term suggests, this is a situation where one team—usually led by a contractor—performs both design and construction work and delivers a finished product to the client, often for a set price. With some projects, this can be an attractive option as long as the design-build company takes the trouble to learn enough about the needs of a theatre to do a creditable job. At a minimum, a design-build contractor should be required to obtain the services of an architect (often required by local regulation) and a theatre consultant and include that cost in the fee. Design-build is usually more appropriate for simple, small facilities.

Other Team Members

Owner's Representative, Architect-of-Record: In addition to the design team and contractor, several additional resources may make the process flow more smoothly, save money or both. An owner's representative can be useful in a complex project where the client does not have the time or expertise to make the many working decisions that go into any building project. This consultant's sole responsibility is to advise the organization and represent its interests in dealings with the design and construction firms. Paid separately by the theatre owner, this position does not benefit financially from any increases to the design/construction budget.

If the primary architectural firm is a recognized theatre design firm or is from a different city or state, it may be both practically and politically useful to have a local architect serve as the architect-of-record on the job. This architect collaborates with the design architect and typically produces the many detailed working drawings and shop drawings called for by the construction firm and its subcontractors. As a licensed architect familiar with local permitting idiosyncrasies and local building officials, the local architect can also be helpful in resolving local code issues when they arise.

Phases of Design and Construction

Assembling the Team and Pre-Design Planning

After a client has investigated and purchased or leased their site, the design process can begin in earnest. The client has many options for determining their design process and consultant team. There are three general strategies, each with its own pros and cons:

1. Hire a prime-lead design and documentation team. This is the most common practice. Usually the prime is an architectural firm. The architectural firm can be contracted so that they take responsibility for all required sub-consultants, permitting, and construction administration. The benefit of this strategy is a streamlined management system for the client, with clear hierarchy and responsibility. The problem with this strategy can be that ultimately all the sub-consultants are accountable and responsible to the prime first, the client second. This can create problems if there are ever issues between the client and the prime. Another implication is typically that the prime requires additional payment for project and sub-consultant management.
2. Hire two complementary teams: one a feasibility and business consulting team to help navigate the construction process, political context, and market feasibility; the other a prime-led design and documentation team. Through having two voices that are both directly contracted to the client, the client can get the benefit of honest and unbiased critique of the process and design from both parties. The detriment with such a team is that pressure is put on the client for any conflict resolution, but this pressure is mitigated by having only two voices.
3. A strategy employed by more and more clients who have construction management experience is to directly contract all consultants to the client, and the client then takes on the management and permitting responsibilities. This can be a significant cost savings strategy if the client truly has the capacity to manage the project. In that case the client also gets the benefit of all consultants only being responsible directly to the client, and the client can have total control. This can also be a total disaster with a client who does not have the relevant management or construction knowledge, potentially miring a project in litigation and escalating costs.

To find an architectural consultant, there are many strategies. For projects using public dollars, a public bidding process with a Request For Proposal (RFP) or Request For Qualifications (RFQ) can be issued by the client for all interested parties. Often, when public money is involved, there can be low-bid requirements, making the client hire the lowest qualified bidder. To ensure that the client gets the quality of consultant they desire, they must carefully craft the RFP and required qualifications. For projects without public money, a client can choose to issue an RFP or simply hire a consultant directly if they already know whom they prefer to work with. For public amenities, some architectural firms will offer reduced fee or pro-bono services for portions or all of the contract.

Another vehicle for selecting a consultant team is the design competition. Design competitions are the cheapest way to get a lot of design ideas for a project. Competitions can be divided into two broad categories: paid and unpaid competitions. Both types are more fully explained in Appendix A.

The Importance of Budget

Even at this early stage, it is imperative that the client develop a straightforward and conservative project budget. The design process needs to take place within a reasonable set of financial expectations without which design teams can waste time on infeasible concepts.

Pre-Design Homework

While gathering a design consultant team, there is background information a client can gather to better facilitate the design process and avoid future snags. Further details about each of these reports is in Appendix A.

- Site survey. A site survey, provided by a licensed surveyor, is required for construction.
- Geotechnical report. A geotechnical report, provided by a licensed geotechnical engineer, is an often-overlooked document that can have major implications for the design, construction and durability of a project.
- Biological survey. A biological survey is usually only

needed for sites with sensitive habitats (such as sites with wetlands) or sites in national parks, state parks, or national forest.
- Project schedule. A clear and specific project schedule developed at the beginning of a project will let the design team plan accordingly. A project schedule can be developed internally or with the advice of the prime consultants. Issues impacting schedule may include permitting processes, required reviews, tendering processes, and construction realities.

Once a design team is assembled and informed, a clear communication strategy with point people for each party should be determined.

Concept Design

The processes described in this section are based on North American standard professional practice. The basic concepts and sequence of events will be very similar throughout the world, although job titles and terminology may vary. In developing parts of the world, government or corporate sponsorship of projects may require significantly different procedures.

The concept design phase is when the 'big moves' of the design and experience should be planned out. What does the facility look like? What is the circulation? What are the approximate square footages of the spaces? How many seats are in the theatre? The client and theatre consultant need to be particularly involved in this stage. If the client has a specific aesthetic or vision, communicating it to the design team will help streamline the process. It is perfectly acceptable for the client to request multiple options for concepts, and to feel comfortable rejecting, critiquing, or questioning the designs.

The client should expect renderings and visualizations of what the project will look like, some broad concepts of the materials involved, and scale of the improvements proposed. Concept design is the freest phase in the design and construction process, and a lively, iterative, creative and informed discussion is the heart of the process. For the rest of the project to flow smoothly, the team should nail down the concept at the end of concept design. A clear vision can guide the rest of the process, and simplify all the future decisions and details.

The cost estimate at the end of concept design is a very inaccurate number, but can provide a ballpark estimate of the project to check against the budget. Typically a 'design contingency' is added to the raw estimate to account for all the items that may be overlooked. Depending on the complexity of the project and how detailed the concept design is, design contingencies can range from 15 to 25 % of the raw estimate at this stage. The raw estimate plus the design contingency and any other contingencies included (such as geotechnical, if no geotechnical report was provided earlier on) together make the concept design cost estimate. It is acceptable for the owner to not accept the concept design until the cost estimate meets or is below the required budget. Construction projects rarely become more affordable during the documentation and construction process, and one of the best cost-control measures a team can have is a decent acceptable estimate at the end of concept design.

Concept design can also be the period that most benefits from community engagement. Depending on the client and site, a community process may or may not be required. Regardless of the requirement, incorporating community feedback at this stage can prevent animosity later in the process. Architects and landscape architects are both capable of managing and determining the best community process for the project. A quality community process can improve the relationship a project has with the community and generate support for the theatre organization. If a community feels collective ownership for a project, they can be one of the greatest supporters and advocates in the future. In addition, a documented community process is helpful for grant applications.

If local building codes or regulations require an entitlement process or an Environmental Impact Report (EIR), concept design is also the stage to secure these approvals and incorporate the mandated feedback.

Schematic Design

In some projects, the schematic design phase is folded into the concept design phase. When schematic design is broken out as a separate phase, it differs from concept design in documentation. A schematic design is typically the first phase of construction documentation. Schematic design takes the concept into drafted form, testing the horizontal and vertical layout of the design.

The client can expect to see scaled, drafted plans, sections, and elevations of the proposed facility. Key and custom details are often included, as is a detailed materials palette with areas demarcated on the plans for different materials and details. At the end of schematic design, the design contingency is generally revised downward. If the design contingency was 25% in concept design, it may be 15% by the end of schematic. Schematic design should be the time to investigate and modify the plan as needed to become a built reality. The client should still feel comfortable providing design direction and critique through reviews during the schematic design phase.

Design Development
After schematic design, the team generally shifts into a substantially more technical mode. Design development is typically when the majority of 'stand-alone' details are generated. At the end of design development, the client can expect the drafted package to identify all the pieces of the project. The design contingency generally drops to approximately 10% at the end of documentation. During design documentation, the client should provide feedback in regard to the materials and details. Revising the 'big moves' of the concept can begin to have significant schedule impacts during design development.

Construction Documents (CD)
Sometimes design documentation is folded into construction documentation. Construction documentation is the phase when all the details of the project are worked out, drafted, and all the required specifications are written. Construction documentation is where the bulk of time is invested in the design and documentation process. This is also the most important stage for the ultimate results of the project. Whatever is in the final drafted drawings and specifications book is what the contractor bids on. The contractor is responsible only for whatever is in those drawings and specifications, and if there are errors or omissions from the package, the contractor can charge change orders for anything with new costs. As a result, the final CD package must be complete and thorough. At the end of construction documentation there is no design contingency, and the cost estimate should provide a number to compare the contractors bids against. Most consultants will use a Quality Assessment Quality Control (QAQC) process of internal review to guarantee the quality of the package. The client has the ultimate authority in accepting the package. The client should provide careful review of the full package, and withhold payment until the package is deemed complete and ready to issue as a tendering package.

Bidding
Typically the client or prime consultant issues a request for bids to eligible contractors. The tendering package usually includes the CDs, specifications, and other relevant information (such as geotechnical report and site survey). The more information provided by the client, the more accurate the bids will be from the contractors. As with the selection of the design team, public projects may require a low bid. In those cases it is vitally important to have detailed requirements for eligibility qualifications. A bad contractor can ruin a project, and bankruptcy can prevent the client from pursuing the contractor to make good on their contract. There are individuals and firms that use this as a business strategy, and a client must be savvy to avoid bad contractors.

Once the contractor is chosen, the contract will legally bind the contractor to complete the terms of the contract and bid documents. Once again, this highlights the importance of high quality and complete CDs and specifications. The contractor can rightfully ask for added payment for any future design changes.

Construction
When the construction bid has been awarded, the actual construction work begins. This is a very exciting time for an organization because plans are finally beginning to materialize, but it can also be a period when a lot of pressure arises from the fact that the clock is now ticking and any mistakes or poor decisions can be costly.

Although the contractor has the primary responsibility for managing the construction of the theatre, it will typically be coordinating the work of the subcontractors that will provide the 'trades,' which include steel, carpentry, mechanical, electrical and plumbing, plus any number of secondary subcontractors covering such areas as excavation, drywall, glazing, roofing, painting, etc. The lead contractor's work process consists of analyzing the designs that have been provided, planning how actually to build them, ordering the necessary materials, fabricating and installing them. This work needs to be orchestrated so that all the subcontractors and myriad parts of the design are executed in the right order and at the right time. Any interruption to this process at any level can slow down or stop the entire train of construction events. If a design is not clear, something doesn't fit, the right materials are not available, or a supplier or subcontractor goes out of business and needs to be replaced—these and dozens of other problems can create havoc. In construction, delays increase costs substantially.

From the lead contractor's point of view, the bid price of the job has been calculated on an efficient flow of work and usually includes a contingency to allow for unforeseen or hidden conditions. The margins have to be very tight in order for the builder to have put forth a competitive enough price to win the job. The builder is entitled to increase the price, however, if the plans that the original price was based on change. Consequently, contractors are on the alert for any opportunity to request a change order with a new price. Since the incentive of winning the contract is no longer an issue, change order costs tend to be high.

In this process, the client and the bid documents have the ultimate authority. Many times, the specifications will call for color samples to be provided for different materials in submittals. In those cases, the prime will pick the color they prefer—it is within the rights of the client to participate in those submittal approvals. The client is also the ultimate authority for all decisions regarding clarifications or changes to the construction plans. The client can negotiate change orders. The implication of these rights is that a well-informed client can simplify the construction process and provide dispute resolution.

This again emphasizes the importance of careful early planning on the part of the organization and its designers and consultants. The owner's representative, discussed above, can be of invaluable assistance throughout the construction process, anticipating and heading off unnecessary change orders and advising the theatre client through the hard decisions.

Planning During Construction

In most cases, theatres will want to begin functioning soon after construction is complete, which means that hiring and training the staff needs to be carefully linked to the construction schedule. In an ideal situation, the staff will be ready just in time for the theatre to open soon after it has been finished. Likewise, equipment and systems that are not part of the building design will need to be ordered and received, ready for installation and training as soon as the staff can occupy the facility. Office equipment, computers, box office systems, concessions equipment, heavy tools or machinery, custodial equipment and supplies all fall into this category. Just as the owner's representative can help avoid log jams and extra costs in the construction of the theatre, the theatre management consultant can assist in orchestrating the approach to the theatre's opening. It is an excellent practice to have a complete project management timetable starting from the time that design is complete and ending with the opening performance, where all these factors are sequenced in the most efficient manner. Problems that can be anticipated and resolved on paper rarely occur in reality.

When Construction Is 'Complete'

The theatre facility will not be ready for occupancy when construction is complete. Several more steps need to be completed before the public can actually attend an event.

- Commissioning: The building and its systems must be commissioned or tested and made ready for operation. Electrical, HVAC (for support spaces), fire safety, toilets and plumbing, and special equipment must all be tested and certified to work properly.
- When construction is substantially complete, the client, architect and builder all tour the facility in a detailed inspection. Notes are made of all items that need to be corrected before the building can be officially declared complete and the builder can be paid his remaining fee. The list of these items is called a 'punch list.' The builder is obligated to complete this before receiving any final monies due.
- The ultimate leverage the client has is this substantial completion—when the terms of the bid documents have been met. Typically a large percentage of the payment to the contractor is held for after acceptance of substantial completion. Usually contractors are hungry for this final payment, and it is near the end of the project when the client will have the greatest leverage for demanding any fixes or negotiating change orders. Once the punch list items are completed, the prime will recommend to the client that the project is complete. The client also has the power to waive punch list items.
- An important strategic consideration in this process is schedule. If the client is under pressure to open

a project, they may be forced into accepting errors from the contractor they would otherwise not accept. Planning a realistic construction schedule and holding the contractor to that schedule are important in the final weeks and months of work when the final fit and finish requires detailed review and follow-up.
- At the end of the project, in addition to the keys, the client can expect a complete set of documents, maintenance manuals, and relevant product information.
- Fire inspection. Even with outdoor theatres, a local fire marshal must formally certify that the facility has been built according to code and can be safely evacuated in an emergency.
- Finally, the client receives a Certificate of Occupancy from the local building inspector. The public is not allowed in the facility until this "C of O" has been awarded, and any insurance coverage will not be valid without one. It should be added that both the fire marshal and building inspector should be involved in any building project very early in the process and invited to tour the facility throughout the construction period. Although it is the responsibility of the designer and the builder to meet all local code requirements, there are invariably gray areas subject to interpretation, and it is important to establish good relationships with the inspectors from the beginning.

Opening the Facility

Organizations will develop their own individual plans to celebrate the opening of their new facilities and there are, of course, consultants who specialize in producing such events. The following guidelines and suggestions may be useful when planning such an event.

- It is more important to open well than to open quickly. A theatre facility earns a great deal of its reputation with its first performances, and a strong opening can be a very effective springboard for a first season. Conversely, a weak opening plagued with technical glitches can be hard to live down for a surprising length of time. For this reason, some theatres opt for a 'soft opening' in which one or several performances are given to a preview audience before the official 'grand' opening. Inviting the construction crew and their families to one such event is a common practice and accomplishes the dual purpose of testing the facility and thanking the workers for their hard work.
- For most theatres an inclusive opening is better than an exclusive one. While donors, the press, and public officials naturally need to be made to feel special and honored, this can be accomplished in a variety of ways by including targeted events during the opening period. It is the general public whose word of mouth will spread the reputation of the theatre the most, so sharing this special time with a wide range of businesses, local organizations, students and the public at large will be appreciated and noted.
- Be careful not to overspend. As with weddings, there is a great temptation to make a big impression and throw a great party, but it usually benefits the ego of the leadership more than the future success of the theatre. Openings should be viewed as break-even events at worst and successful fundraising events at best.
- If the facility can do different things in addition to producing a play (such as hosting dinners and receptions, giving tours, holding educational events or demonstrations) the opening events should be careful to showcase each of those types of functions. Every space in which an event can be held should be used in a successful opening.
- If the theatre plans a donor wall where the founding donors will be permanently honored, have a replica of it when the theatre opens rather than the finished wall. Potential donors may be motivated to make a contribution when they see how fine the facility really is, and this may encourage them to donate in time to be recognized as a founder. Some theatres have waited a full year before installing the permanent recognition to take full advantage of these last-minute donors.
- Every aspect of every part of the event should be planned and stage managed in meticulous detail. Even when nothing is left to chance, the unexpected will still occur and management needs to be ready for all eventualities. This is particularly true, it goes without saying, in outdoor theatre!

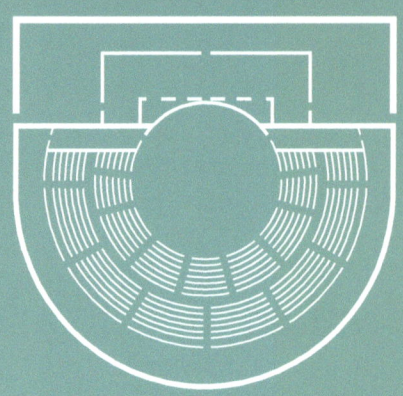

Chapter 7

Conclusions

Conclusions

As we noted in the introduction to this book, the number of outdoor performances around the world has probably never been higher than at the present time. Outdoor theatre shares most of the challenges faced by all theatre, including rising costs, changing tastes and competition from other entertainment forms, particularly the current tsunami of digital content. It also has several unique advantages and challenges that can be emphasized or mitigated as needed. Achieving a successful facility design will be an important means to that end.

Advantages

Outdoor theatre is particularly accessible to the general public. Whether admission is charged or not, there is a democratic quality to open-air events and theatres without walls. Performances, by necessity, take place during the seasonable times of the year, which are associated with vacations, outdoor recreation and some level of relaxation from the usual demands of work. In these months, families and friends look for ways and times to be together. While indoor theatres are often reducing their programs during the height of summer, outdoor theatres are flourishing. They generally have lower overhead costs than indoor theatres, so are able to offer less expensive tickets, further encouraging family attendance. Because of these factors, outdoor audiences tend to be more representative of a cross-section of the population. The point of attending is to have a good time, be entertained and share the experience with friends and family. These advantages can combine to make attending an outdoor production both a satisfying and authentic experience.

Challenges

One of the biggest challenges that outdoor theatres face is that several other leisure-time industries have similar advantages. Cruise lines, resorts, and theme parks all target the leisure time market and have invested millions in product and market development that theatres cannot expect to match. None of them, however, can be accessed as spontaneously and inexpensively as outdoor theatre. But the existence and reputation of these forms of entertainment puts a great deal of pressure on theatres to raise the quality of their facilities and productions. Thirty or even 15 years ago, audiences experiencing a bad sound system, inadequate lighting or badly maintained toilets might have shrugged it off without a second thought. Today, these shortcomings can be expected to show up in tweets before the play is over and customer reviews on TripAdvisor by the next day. The social media's ability to affect customer opinion and word of mouth is a powerful tool that can have immediate and lasting influence on a theatre—for good or ill.

Competition for leisure time is also a significant challenge. Today there are more entertainment products available than at any previous time in history, and there is no end in sight to their continued proliferation. This suggests that outdoor theatres need to offer a variety of shows to their audiences where possible. In this report we have recommended the full or partially roofed amphitheatre as a model for new or renovated theatres for these reasons:

- It provides superior sound and lighting production capacity.
- It accommodates changing shows far more easily.
- The protection from the elements helps prevent cancellations and is more comfortable for the audiences.

Finally, we see that there is a tremendous range of outdoor theatre production today. From volunteer community theatres to highly sophisticated spectacles, outdoor venues operate throughout the world. The Institute of Outdoor Theatre's mission is to support, inform and engage these organizations and promote their work to audiences and supporters. While the performers and the audience are always the most important ingredients for any theatre experience, we know that the facilities that bring them together also play a vital role in their ultimate success and sustainability.

Fig 102 / Oregon Shakespeare Festival, Ashland, OR. *A Midsummer Night's Dream* (2013).

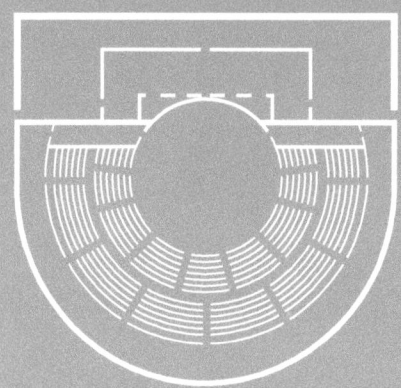

Appendices

Appendix A: Further Notes on Design and Construction Process

Site Survey

A site survey, provided by a licensed surveyor, is required for construction. If a survey is provided at the beginning of the design process, the consultant team will 'get real' with the designs much faster and perform more efficiently for the client. A quality site survey will include the property lines, 1-foot interval contours, spot elevations at high points and low points, spot elevations on a grid (30' by 30' for large uniform sites, 10' by 10' for varied or small sites), tree trunks with diameter measurements for trees to remain near or in the proposed improvements, edge of forest, boundaries of water bodies, and the footprint of any existing structures with finished floor elevations and doorways.

Geotechnical Report

A geotechnical report, provided by a licensed geotechnical engineer, is an often overlooked document that can have major implications for the design, construction, and durability of a project. A geotechnical report will provide recommendations for construction, such as what should be required for effective compaction of soils prior to construction, bedrock issues, seismic issues, and groundwater issues. Sometimes moving a facility slightly on a site can save significant costs by avoiding some subsurface obstruction or weakness. Having this information at the beginning of a project can remove these mysteries and prevent potential huge costs in additional reinforcement or change orders later in the process. There are sites and locations where a geotechnical report will be unnecessary, and an experienced local construction manager, landscape architect, or architect can advise on the need. In general, sites in areas with steep terrain, variable soils, caves, historic flood plains, exposed bedrock, or clay soil all generally benefit from a geotechnical report.

Biological Survey

A biological survey is usually needed only for sites with sensitive habitats (such as sites with wetlands) or sites in national parks, state parks, or national forest. A biological survey will document the existing habitats and species composition. In some states a biological survey will be required for the EIR prior to entitlement of permitting. In other states, no biological survey is required. Usually a local department of fish and game, biological consulting company, environmental engineer, or landscape architect can advise on the needs for a particular site.

Design Competitions

- Paid competitions. The client pays a small fee to a select group of firms to develop their ideas. Paid competitions can be written so that the winner gets the contract, or not. Paid competitions can have an RFQ process beforehand to solicit a group from which the client may select a shortlist for participation.
- Unpaid competitions. Unpaid competitions are typically open to anyone who meets the eligibility requirements for submitting. If a client just wants ideas, the competition can be open to all—including students. If a client wants participation from firms that can actually deliver the project, then eligibility requirements can be written with the requirements in mind. Generally, if a contract is not guaranteed to the winner of the competition, a significant pool of money will attract greater participation. If a contract is guaranteed to the winner, then the prize can be smaller or nonexistent.

The quality of results from a competition is generally dependent on how well organized and advertised the competition brief is. A quality competition brief will include a site survey, existing photographs, information on the proposed program and local context, and clear submission requirements. Posting the competition on the hosting organization's webpage, and sharing the competition brief with state organizations such as the AIA (American Institute of Architecture and ASLA (American Society of Landscape Architects), and on sites such as Archinect, ArchDaily, Bustler, and World Landscape Architecture, will attract greater participation than a passively advertised competition.

Appendix B: Schedule for a Typical 1000-Seat Outdoor Theatre

		Net Sq. Feet (nsf)	Notes
A100	**Public Spaces**		
101	Entrance Pavilion	2,500	2.5 nsf per seat
102	Auditorium sound & light locks		in gross
103	Concessions	500	
104	Concessions storage	100	
105	Public restrooms (male)	480	4 toilets and 8 urinals
106	Public restrooms (female)	1,100	22 toilets
107	Front-of-house storage	180	
108	Box office - sales	180	3 stations
109	Box office - administration	180	
110	Office - house manager	140	
111	Usher locker room	100	
A200	**Performance Space**		
201	Auditorium	10,000	10 nsf per seat
202	Stage and wings	4,000	40' x 100' wide
203	Stage apron	160	60' proscenium opening
204	Stage crossover	440	8' wide (minimum)
205	Control booth	100	
206	Booth - production stage manager	40	
207	Followspot booth(s)	180	
208	In-house sound control	160	
209	Dimmer room	120	
210	Sound rack room	80	
211	FOH catwalk		in gross
212	Grid		in gross
A300	**Performer Support**		
301	Performer waiting area	500	covered outdoor area
302	Dressing room - 4 person	220	sink, makeup stations, toilet, sofa
303	Dressing room - 4 person	220	sink, makeup stations, toilet, sofa
304	Dressing room - 8 person	300	makeup, sink, toilets, lockers, chairs, etc.
305	Dressing room - 8 person	300	makeup, sink, toilets, lockers, chairs, etc.
306	Dressing room - 24 person	800	makeup, sink, toilets, lockers, chairs, etc.
307	Dressing room - 24 person	800	makeup, sink, toilets, lockers, chairs, etc.
308	Wardrobe / Quick-change	80	
309	Showers - male	140	
310	Showers - female	140	

Appendix B: Schedule for a Typical 1000-Seat Outdoor Theatre Continued

		Net Sq. Feet (nsf)	Notes
A400	**Stage Support**		
401	Office - stage management	160	
402	Office - visiting production	120	
403	Production staff breakroom	180	
404	Backstage restroom (male)	180	3 units (H/C accessible)
405	Backstage restroom (female)	180	3 units (H/C accessible)
406	Storage - production scenery	500	
407	Storage - production props	180	
408	Storage - general	300	
409	Storage - musical instruments	120	
410	Performer canteen and storage	140	

A500	**Scenery and Costume Shops**		
501	Scenery shop	800	
502	Office - technical director	120	
503	Storage - tools	60	
504	Storage - paint	60	
505	Storage - hazardous materials	60	
506	Storage - materials	120	
507	Storage - firearms and effects	60	
508	Costume shop	800	
509	Office - costumer	120	
510	Storage - materials	180	
511	Laundry and dyeing	180	

A600	**Rehearsal Room**		
601	Rehearsal room	2,800	40' x 80' x 16' minimum clear height
602	Storage - rehearsal room	280	
603	Storage - piano	100	

A700	**Administrative Offices**		
701	Office - executive director	200	off-site?
702	Office - reception and waiting	160	off-site?
703	Office - staff	140	off-site?
704	Office - staff	140	off-site?
705	Work stations (4 @ 60 nsf)	240	off-site?
706	Conference room	300	off-site?
707	Office equipment and supplies	120	off-site?

		Net Sq. Feet (nsf)	Notes
A800	**Services**		
801	Storage - general	160	
802	Housekeeping closets	120	3 @ 40 nsf
803	Trash/Recycling storage & disposal	-	in gross
804	Loading dock	-	in gross
805	Office - maintenance	160	
806	Groundskeeping - garage	500	
	Total Net Square Feet	34,280	

Appendix C: Image Sources and Attributions

- Chapter 1 Title: BreeAnne Clowdus, Serenbe Playhouse, The Ugly Duckling
- Fig. 1: Славен Косановић, CC-BY-SA 3.0 License
- Fig. 2: Jerzy Strzelecki, CC-BY-SA 3.0 License
- P. 11 Top to bottom: The Sound of Music 2013, Regent's Park Open Air Theatre, Photo: David Jensen; Barry Moore, Gensler; Iroquois Amphitheater; Hudson Valley Shakespeare Festival; Petr Hasal, The Revolving Theatre Cesky Krumlov, CC-BY-SA License
- Chapter 2 Title: Sidney B. Cushing Memorial Amphitheatre, Robin McNally
- Fig. 3: Engraving after Carl Emil Doepler (1905). Source from Holzstich original aus einer Zeitschrift von 1860
- Fig. 4: Swarthmore College
- Fig. 5: Daniel Ramirez, CC-BY-2.0 Generic License
- Fig. 6: Creative Commons, CC-BY-SA 3.0 License
- Fig. 7: Land for sale sign, Steve Fareham CC-BY-SA 2.0 License
- Fig. 8: U.S. Army Corps of Engineers, CC-BY 2.0 Generic License
- Fig. 9: Chris Hardy, CC-BY-SA License
- Fig. 10: Shoelace Park Master Plan, Bronx, New York, Image courtesy of Mathews Nielsen Landscape Architects, P.C. (MNLA) with Bronx River Alliance
- Fig. 11: Barry Moore, Gensler
- Chapter 3 Title: Bengt Sjostrom Starlight Theatre, Greg Murphy
- Fig. 12: D. H. Ramsey Library, Special Collections, University of North Carolina at Asheville
- Fig. 13: Daniel Baker, CC-BY-ND 2.0 Generic License
- Fig. 14: Michael Hardy
- Fig. 15: Billy Bass, The Stephen Foster Story
- Fig. 16: Ravinia/Patrick Gipson
- Fig. 17: Better Than Bacon, CC-BY-SA 2.0 Generic License
- Fig. 18: Lisa Ludwig, Shakespeare in Delaware Park
- Fig. 19: The Minack Theatre Library
- Fig. 20: The Stephen Foster Story
- Fig. 21: Elm Shakespeare Company
- Fig. 22: BreeAnne Clowdus, Serenbe Playhouse, The Sleepy Hollow Experience
- Fig. 23: Chris Hardy
- Fig. 24: Karl Hugh, copyright Utah Shakespeare Festival, 2011
- Fig. 25: Karl Hugh, copyright Utah Shakespeare Festival, 2013
- Fig. 26: The Lost Colony
- Fig. 27: Carissa Dixon, American Players Theatre
- Fig. 28: Used by permission of Shenandoah University
- Chapter 4 Title: Zorlack, CC-BY-2.0 Generic License
- Fig. 29: Chris Hardy, CC-BY-SA-2.0-DE License
- Fig. 30: EJ Posselius, CC-BY-SA-2.0 Generic License
- Fig. 31: Photo by Brian Stethem, Kingsmen Shakespeare Company
- Fig. 32: Leroy Gibbons, Miller Outdoor Theatre
- Fig. 33: TonyTheTiger, CC-BY-SA 3.0 License
- Fig. 34: John Picken, CC-BY-SA 2.0 Generic License
- Fig. 35: TonyTheTiger, CC-BY-SA 3.0 License
- Chapter 5 Title: Delacorte Theater, Tammy Shell
- P. 57: Top to bottom: The Sound of Music, 2013, Regent's Park Open Air Theatre, Photo: David Jensen; Barry Moore, Gensler; Iroquois Amphitheater; Hudson Valley Shakespeare Festival; Petr Hasal, The Revolving Theatre Cesky Krumlov, CC-BY-SA License
- Fig. 36: Barry Moore, Gensler
- Fig. 37: Barry Moore, Gensler
- Fig. 38, 39: Lee Bennett, CC-BY-NC-SA 2.0 Generic License
- Fig. 40: Michael Hardy
- Fig. 41: DKM Photography, Idaho Shakespeare Festival
- Fig. 42-45: Tecumseh!, The Scioto Society, Inc.
- Fig. 46-49: Right page – Top left to bottom right: Gigi_nyc, CC-BY-NC-ND 2.0 Generic License; Rebecca Marks, CC-BY-NC-SA 2.0 Generic License; Brianac37, CC-BY 2.0 Generic License; Tammy Shell
- Fig. 50-52: Tuacahn Center for the Arts, Courtesy of The Inn at St. George, InnStGeorge.com; AdamRC98, CC-BY-SA 3.0 License
- Fig. 53: The Sound of Music, 2013, Regent's Park Open Air Theatre, photo: David Jensen
- Fig. 54: Barry Moore, Gensler
- Fig. 55: Barry Moore, Gensler
- Fig. 56-58: Barry Moore, Gensler
- Fig. 59-61: Left: Kendl-Bühne Wuhlheide, CC-BY-SA 3.0 License; middle: CC-BY-SA License; background: La Citta Vita, CC-BY-SA 2.0 Generic License
- Fig. 62: Barry Moore, Gensler
- Fig. 63: Barry Moore, Gensler

- Fig. 64: Barry Moore, Gensler
- Fig. 65: Barry Moore, Gensler
- Fig 66-68: left: Schlaier CC-BY-SA License; bottom: Sourav Niyogi CC-BY-SA 3.0 License; right: John Tramper, Shakespeare's Globe
- Fig. 69: Leroy Gibbons, Miller Outdoor Theatre
- Fig. 70: Ravinia/Patrick Gipson
- Fig. 71: Ravinia/Patrick Gipson
- Fig. 72: Iroquois Amphitheater
- Fig. 73: Wikimedia Commons
- Fig. 74: Karel Dujardin, Commedia dell'Arte Show, 1657
- Fig. 75: Hudson Valley Shakespeare Festival
- Fig. 76: John Western, The San Francisco Shakespeare Festival
- Fig. 77: Photo Blimp, Vancouver, Bard on the Beach Shakespeare Festival
- Fig. 78: Michael Doucett, Lucia Neare's Theatrical Wonders
- Fig. 79: Leena Klemelä, CC-BY-SA 3.0 License
- Fig. 80: Petr Hasal, The Revolving Theatre Cesky Krumlov, CC-BY-SA License
- Fig. 81: Barry Moore, Gensler
- Fig. 82: Barry Moore, Gensler
- Fig. 83: © 2013 Paul R. Kennedy, UC Irvine New Swan Theater
- Fig. 84, 85: Lucerne Festival Ark Nova
- Fig. 86-89: Greg Murphy, Bengt Sjostrom Starlight Theatre
- Fig. 90-93: Weill Hall, Sonoma State University. left to right: images courtesy of SWA, photographers Jonnu Singleton, Tom Fox, and Zachary Davis
- Fig. 94: ©www.thewalkingtheatrecompany.com by permission of Sadie Dixon-Spain
- Fig. 95-101 Eric Bunge, nARCHITECTS
- Chapter 6 Title: James Crookall CC-BY-SA 2.0 Generic License
- Chapter 7 Title: Laurie Malton for Shakespeare WA (Western Australia)
- Fig. 102: T. Charles Erickson, Oregon Shakespeare Festival, 2013, A Midsummer Night's Dream

Index

access to stage area, 38
Actors' Equity, 38
American Institute of Architecture, 134
American Players Theatre, *44*
American Society of Landscape Architects, 134
Americans with Disabilities Act, 36, 49
amphitheatres, inflatable, *108*
amphitheatres, rotating, *104*
Angel, Eugene, 65
ArchDaily, 134
Archinect, 134
Ark Nova, *108, 109*
Auerbach Pollock Friedlander, 112

backstage requirements, 38–41
    crossover, 41
    dressing rooms, 38–39
    green room, 40
    technical spaces, 40
Bard on the Beach, 98, *100*–101
Bengt Sjostrom Starlight Theatre, 90, *110, 111*
Berry, Wendell, 25
biological survey, 134
box office, 30
Bravura Architecture, 96
Bronx River Alliance, 23
brownfields, 21
building new theatre, 118–127
    bidding, 125
    client and design team, 120–121
    concept design, 124
    construction, 125–127
    construction documents, 125
    design-build, 121
    opening facility, 127
    phases of design and construction, 122–123
    program, 120–121
    schematic design, 124–125
Bunge, Eric, 116
Bustler, 134

Casarella, Gary, 35
Cemil Topuzlu Open-Air Theatre, *17*
Český Krumlov, *105*

Cirque du Soleil, 98
commedia dell-arte, *98*
Comprehensive Environmental Response, Compensation, and Liability Act, 21
concessions, 32
Conquistador, 41
construction, 120–127, 134
    bidding, 125
    biological survey, 134
    client and design team, 120–121
    concept design, 124
    construction documents, 125
    design-build, 121
    geotechnical report, 134
    opening facility, 127
    phases of design and, 122–123
    program, 120–121
    schematic design, 124–125
    site survey, 134
control booth, 34
crossover, 41

Delacorte Theater, 69
design, 24, 118–127
    bidding, 125
    concept design, 124
    construction, 125–127
    construction documents, 125
    low-impact, 24
    low-maintenance, 24
    of new theatre, 118–127
        client and design team, 120–121
        design-build, 121
        program, 120–121
    opening facility, 127
    phases of design and construction, 122–123
    schematic design, 124–125
design competitions, 134
draperies, 51, 51
dressing rooms, 38–39
Dujardins, Karel, *98*

Eckert, Allan W., 66
Environmental Impact Report, 20
Environmental Impact Review, 134

Environmental Protection Agency, 19
equipment, 46–53
    design and procurement, 52
    lighting, *48*, 48–49
    off-season storage, 52
    rigging, 50, *50*
    sound and communication, 49, *49*
    stage draperies, 51, *51*

facility, 26–45
    box office, 30
    concessions, 32
    control booth, 34
    entry pavilion, 30
    front-of-house requirements, 28–30, *31*, 32–36
    gift shop, 33
    parking, 29
    seating and sightlines, 34–36
    stage and backstage requirements, 38–41
    toilet facilities, 34
Federal Bureau of Alcohol, Tobacco and Firearms, 40
Federal Emergency Management Agency, 19
flood plains, 19
floor, stage, 43
Forest Pavilion, *116, 117*
front-of-house requirements, 28–30, *31*, 32–36

Gehry, Frank, 51
geotechnical report, 134
gift shop, 33
Globe Theatre, 82, *90, 91*, 114
green room, 40

Halprin, Lawrence, 17
Hegel-Cantarella, Luke, 106
Hill Country Arts Foundation, 79
Hoang, Mimi, 116
Holabird, John Augur, 95
Howard, John, 16
Hudson Valley Shakespeare Festival, *99*
Hunter, Kermit, 63

Idaho Shakespeare Festival, *64–65*
Idaho Shakespeare Festival Amphitheater and Habitat
    Reserve, 65

inflatable amphitheatres, *108*
Institute of Outdoor Theatre, 8, 62, 130
Iroquois Amphitheater, 82, *96–97*
Iroquois Park, 96
Isozaki, Arata, 108

Jay Pritzker Pavilion, *51*
Jensen, Jens, 16

Kapoor, Anish, 108
Kingsmen Shakespeare Company, *50*
Kirkegaard, Lawrence, 112

Lake Tahoe Shakespeare Festival, 32
landscape, stewardship of, 25
landscape design, cost-effective, 24
LeMosh, Joseph Michal, 65
Leopold, Aldo, 25
lighting, 44–45, *48*, 48–49
Lost Colony, The, *29, 43*
Lucerne Festival, 108
Lucia Neare's Theatrical Wonders, *102–103*

March, Werner, 81
Marley, Bob, 81
Masdi Art Festival, 116
Mathews Nielsen Landscape Architects, 23
McGraw-Hill Construction, 25
Millennium Park, 51
Miller Outdoor Theatre, *50, 92–93*
Minack Theatre, 24, *37*, 62
Moore, Barry, 79
Mountainside Theatre, *28, 63*

nARCHITECTS, 116
New Swan Theater, 90, *106–107*
new theatre, designing and building, 118–127
    bidding, 125
    client and design team, 120–121
    concept design, 124
    construction, 125–127
    construction documents, 125
    design-build, 121
    facility design, 120

opening facility, 127
phases of design and construction, 122–123
program, 120–121
schematic design, 124–125

Oberammergau, 16, *16*
Olmsted, Frederick Law, 35, 96
open wall theatre, *112, 113*
orchestra pit, 45, *45*
Oregon Shakespeare Festival, *131*
outdoor productions, types, 12
outdoor theatre, 10–11, *11*, 13, 16, 54–117, 130
    advantages, 130
    challenges, 130
    early 20th century, 16
    hybrid theatres, *11, 57,* 104–113
    open stage with open amphitheatre, *11, 57,* 58–62, *59–61, 63–73*
    relationship to site, 16
    roofed stage and amphitheatre, *11, 57,* 82–97, *83–85, 87–97*
    roofed stage with open amphitheatre, 11, 57, 74–81, *75–79*
    and seasons, 13
    temporary theatres, *11, 57,* 98–103
    types, 54–117

pageant wagon, *98*
Papp, Joseph, 69
parking, 29
performance equipment, 46–53
    design and procurement, 52
    lighting, *48,* 48–49
    off-season storage, 52
    rigging, 50, *50*
    sound and communication, 49, *49*
    stage draperies, 51, *51*
performance planning, 12–13
Public Theater, 69
Pyynikki Summer Theatre, *104*

Ravinia Pavilion, *94–95*
Rawn, William, 112
Red Rocks Amphitheatre, 62

Regent's Park Open Air Theatre, *72–73*
repertory, 12
restrooms, 34
retractable roof, *110, 111*
rigging, 50, *50*
Robinson, Brian, 65
Roman Theatre at Bosra, *9*
rotating amphitheatres, 104

San Francisco Shakespeare Festival, *99*
Scott Outdoor Amphitheater, Swarthmore College, *17*
Sears, Thomas W., 17
seating and sightlines, 34–36
Serenbe Playhouse, *41*
Shakespeare in Delaware Park, *35*
Shakespeare in the Park, *68–69*
Shakespeare Theatre, 110
Shakespeare's Globe, 90
Shoelace Park, *23*
Sigmund Stern Recreation Grove, *17*
site, 14–25
    adjacent landowners, 20
    assets, 22
    brownfields, 21
    comfort, 21
    design principles, 17
    existing structures, 20
    hydrology, 20–21
    orientation, 20
    problems, 19–20
        endangered species habitat, 20
        expansive soil, 19
        flood plains, 19
        high water table, 19
        incompatible zoning, 20
        liquefaction zones, 20
        overly steep or flat sites, 19
        shallow bedrock, 19
        wetlands, 19
    selection, 18
    survey, 134
    variables to consider, *21*
site-specific productions, 114
Smith-Ritch Point Theatre, *25, 78, 79*

sound and communication, 49, *49*
stage, 38, *42*, 42–45
    access to, 38
    diagram, *42*
    lighting positions, 44–45
stage draperies, 51, *51*
stage floor, 43
Stephen Foster Story, The, *31*, 43
Stern Grove Festival, 17
stewardship of landscape, 25
Stoker, Leslie A., 71
Studio Gang Architects, 110
Sugarloaf Mountain Amphitheatre, 66
summer stock, 12
SWA Group, 112

Tecumseh!, 24, *66, 67*
tenting, 86
Texas!, 24
Theatre of Dionysus Eleuthereus, *8*
Tuacahn Center for the Arts, *70–71*
types of outdoor productions, 12

United States Geological Survey, 20
Unto These Hills, 24, *28*, *31*, *63*
Utah Shakespeare Festival, *43*
Utah Shakespeare Theatre, 110
Uysal, Nahid, 17

Vanier Park, *100–101*
vernacular theatre installation, *116, 117*

Waldbühne, *80–81*
Walking Theatre Company, 114, *115*
Waugh, Frank A., 16
Weill Hall, Sonoma State University, *112, 113*
Werlin, Eugene, 92
wetlands, 19
Works Progress Administration, 96
World Landscape Architecture, 134

Yücel, Nihad, 17

www.ingramcontent.com/pod-product-compliance
Lightning Source LLC
Chambersburg PA
CBHW041525220426
43670CB00002B/28